INTERIOR
WHO'S WHO IN

TEXT BY CAROLYNNE MURPHY
EDITED BY MICHAEL MURPHY

The author is indebted to each contributing designer and photographer. Every effort has been made to correctly acknowledge all credits and contacts within *Interior Elite's* Directory. Any error or omission is a genuine mistake and entirely unintentional on the part of the author.

Distributed by

Art Books International

1 Stewart's Court

220 Stewart's Road

London SW8 4UD

United Kingdom

Tel: 020 7720 1503

Fax: 020 7720 3158

E-mail: sales@art-bks.com

First published in 2001 by Carolynne Murphy

Copyright © Carolynne Murphy

The right of Carolynne Murphy to be identified as the author of this work has been asserted in accordance with the Copyright, Designs and Patents Act 1988.

A catalogue record for this book is available from the British Library.

ISBN 0 9539575 0 0

DESIGN AND ART DIRECTION BY FIONA FORSYTH PHOTOGRAPHY SUPPLIED BY DESIGNERS IN PROFILE REPRODUCTION AND PRINTING BY THE HYWAY GROUP IN LONDON

CAROLYNNE MURPHY

INTERIOR ELITE
WHO'S WHO IN DESIGN

A GALLERY OF PERSONALITIES FROM THE WORLD OF INTERIORS

WITH A FOREWORD BY ALLEN SHEPPARD
THE RIGHT HONOURABLE LORD SHEPPARD OF DIDGEMERE, KCVO

IN ASSOCIATION WITH

London First

London First Centre

THE INWARD INVESTMENT AGENCY
FOR LONDON

CONTENTS

WHY?

Each of us has an immortal memory.

For me, there was a moment in 1997 when writing took on new meaning.

I was profiling a designer in Hong Kong for an international publication. He was part of a new generation from the world of interiors whose celebrity status had pushed him to the forefront. In his eyes, I was a necessary evil. He saw hills and mountains between us.

Why would I climb onto his observation deck to view his way of seeing?
Why should I unscramble the link between a spontaneous connection he had made by touching a hand-woven fabric in Thailand and the inspiration it provided for his latest New York interior?

He cancelled many meetings before we finally got together. But when we published, instead of damning me, he called with his thanks. He said our words had crossed borders and put him 'in touch'. Not just with other people but with his own art.

Above all else, I hope *Interior Elite* puts you in touch with some true artists. The stuff of its pages is relationships. Relationships between people, places, time, culture, objects and nature. It is my way of drawing it all together and bringing you in closer. All passion, beauty and individuality, design is a language worth sharing.

What mattered to me most was being able to paint these very independent, very skilled, very, very extraordinary artists as I found them. Many designers register as a small blip, working out of unglamorous studios to produce interiors for the richest of the rich. And whilst artists have museums to preserve their work, designers have clients; private individuals who covet their magnificent spaces behind closed doors.

Studying the work of these artisans was part of learning to see, to hear, to touch, to feel and not to feel, and to write. It connected me with what they are doing as designers - that is, saying something fresh and taking risks. I didn't want to stand on any fierce hearts and tried to let the art affect me on a sub-conscious level.

There was always something new to get over. Even when you're crossing a creative desert it's possible to reach out to someone. You can connect with your mind. I learnt through osmosis, lessons about deliberation and spontaneity, about passion and the role of art in history.

Since cross-references and influences arrive at different times designers have diverse ways of seeing. But each is united in the belief that design must look forward, look back and look around. Change is the constant. Each spectacular invention disrupts the status quo, causing us to look for ways to make things appropriate and pertinent to the way we live, the problems we each face, the values we hold dear. True design innovation is less a quest for newness and more a search for relevance.

Design is an instinctive environment: it is about objects of desire, about impulse and attraction, about creating a unique synergy that sets off a chemical reaction. A kind of dance takes place between a designer and his interior.

With each profile, I was building an edifice - a structure within which emotions and ideas can live. Every architect, designer and decorator was asked for exactly the same contribution: time and effort to show what makes each personality tick. The result is a gallery where people can visit - for reference, ideas, thoughts and dreams.

The book falls into seven sections that could be rearranged like the walls of an exhibition. It contains nearly forty doorways through which you can enter. Constructed like London's Millennium Eye, it is an observation deck; designed to help you see things from a new perspective. You can climb very high to get an overview of the world of interiors, but if your head has been in the clouds for too long, there are elevators designed to bring you back down to ground level. Each designer's story is a separate apartment and yet, in the passions they all share, they are connected by common walls and pathways.

Interior Elite is intended to be different: in its style, its variety and its energy. It blends information with fantasy. It is a celebration of designers who, by following their own visions, challenge us to rethink ours.

Design permeates every aspect of life; it is multi-faceted and elusive, a complex mix of the creative and the practical, an instrument of innovation, effectiveness and expression.

In London we are justifiably proud of our design heritage and our reputation as a global leader in this industry. London has the highest concentration of design firms, designer-producers, advertising agencies and architectural practices in the world employing an estimated 95,000 people.

They are part of a much larger group of cultural and creative industries in Greater London which generate over £25 billion every year for our economy as well as providing a strong nucleus for a growing and professional industry in other parts of the UK.

London is also a world centre of architectural and design education courses : 50 at vocational level, 90 at first degree level and 60 at post-graduate level. The city also helps to market design on a global basis and each year 36 design-related trade exhibitions and events are held in London.

The design industries are, therefore, an important part of our economy; providing jobs and exporting services and expertise. Designers are also in the vanguard of setting trends, not least in spotting the potential in previously run-down areas of our cities. Covent Garden and Clerkenwell in London are two good examples.

London First and London First Centre, the sister organisations whose job it is to promote London, generate inward investment and support existing industries, are acutely conscious of the important role the creative industries play in the life of our capital and in the rest of the UK.

Through the London Development Partnership, we contributed towards a study which is helping us to shape a strategy which will ensure that London maintains its position as the creative capital of the world and, moving forward, we will be placing a great deal of emphasis on this initiative.

One of the key issues highlighted in the report was the need for the design industry to raise its profile at home and internationally as well as the need for it to take more credit for its outstanding achievements. It is with great pleasure, therefore, that I commend to you *Interior Elite*, a showcase for many of London and the UK's top interior designers and their outstanding art.

I am confident that this book will play an important part in promoting our design excellence further at home and overseas and I thank everyone who contributed to its creation.

The Right Honourable Lord Sheppard of Didgemere, KCVO
Chairman of London First

PHOTOGRAPHY

PHOTOGRAPHY

PHOTOGRAPHY

DAVID MLINARIC

DAVID MLINARIC

IT IS A HOT SUMMER'S DAY. THE BEACH IS
NOISY AND CROWDED. A HOLIDAY HAZE HANGS
RELAXED AND HAPPY. SMILING FACES TURN IN
UNISON MAGNETISED BY A BECKONING SEA -
APART FROM ONE SMALL BOY TURNED THE
OTHER WAY. HIS NAME IS DAVID MLINARIC AND
HE IS COUNTING THE WINDOWS ON THE
BUILDING BEHIND.

DESIGN REDISCOVERY

DAVID MLINARIC

David Mlinaric is Britain's most respected designer. Back in 1958, it was Mlinarics' teenage instinct that guided him from a prestigious path of study at London's Bartlett School of Architecture and led him into a new world of interiors. Mlinaric was concerned by that period's destruction of old buildings and disillusioned by their architectural replacements; he has since dedicated his working life to the research and resurrection of Britain's built heritage. His existing partnership, Mlinaric, Henry & Zervudachi Limited was founded in 1989 to provide empathetic interior design and decoration, often in historic buildings, for private clients and commercial or institutional organisations. Past projects include London's National Gallery and Wellcome Building in addition to the three principal heritage buildings of the Foreign and Commonwealth Office; their Embassies in Paris, Brussels and Washington. Based in London, Paris and New York, the practice's current project portfolio includes Castello di Fighine, Tuscany, Italy; houses in Toronto, London and New York; Serlby Hall, Nottinghamshire; The English Primary Galleries at The Victoria & Albert Museum; The Royal Opera House, Covent Garden; The National Portrait Gallery, London and Hoare's Bank, London. David Mlinaric selected two projects to reflect his design profile: Spencer House and Beningbrough Hall. Spencer House, now entering its fourth century, was built between 1756-1766 for John, first Earl Spencer, an ancestor of Diana, Princess of Wales (1961-97). It is one of the finest aristocratic private palaces to survive in London and over 100 craftspeople, including Mlinaric, have been involved in its meticulous restoration. Beningbrough Hall, in Yorkshire, represents Mlinaric's historically knowledgeable and respectful work for the National Trust.

I thought that I knew what to expect from the great restorer of Britain's built heritage, but David Mlinaric turns out to be a puzzle. Once he allowed me to set about researching the projects that reflect his almost 40 years of design narrative, I uncover the self-portrait of an honest artisan rather than a forger of old masters. Mlinaric has spent his life exploring a sense of detachment in a crowded world. His gift is an instinct that he cannot ignore. Silent buildings scream at him, compelling him to make sense of their sensibilities: order, balance and harmony. In the beginning, Mlinaric's work was personal; he was intrigued by his own memories of demon bombsites and architectural decay. But now, supported by bodies like English Heritage, he has conquered past nightmares and reaches out with enthused empathy to protect the decorative art found within meaningful architecture. His mission has made a difference; his design influence surrounds us all. David Mlinaric is the answer for passionate individuals with fine houses and the dedicated money to release architectural splendour. We are talking in his study based within his Chelsea office. It is a respectable refuge amongst the pearly set of other eminently placed London designers. But there is nothing pretentious about the Mlinaric domain or the great arranger who faces me today. His room illuminates a great character rather than the grandeur of his prestigious portfolio. There are no trophies on display; no gilt framed Turner landscapes or uncomfortable antiques. For me it is an intriguing den worth exploring and together we appreciate his most precious souvenir of Spencer House; it is a dog-eared postcard pinned unceremoniously to the wall. The atmosphere is charged solely by his presence and Mlinaric, clad today in black Levi's and statement jewellery, appears to be an artist at ease.

An Interview

Can a word describe what you do?

I am a decorator! Ha, that loaded word, but you can't go through life pondering a mere word. Nobody has put a finger on the right name to describe what we all do. What we do is unspecific. Sometimes we re-work an entire building and sometimes we fit the lining paper in a client's desk.

Can a word describe how you do it?

Commitment. I never cast on anything to cast off. This is a serious business. It is less of a love match and more of an arranged marriage; the approach is professional, planned and mechanical. I commit to the way that people conduct their lives and my own fascination with buildings. I am concerned with the arrangements for breakfast, lunch and dinner. I have never been into a room, no matter how ugly, and not been interested in the way it was arranged.

Can you describe your design approach?

I've been editing rooms all my life. I start instinctively and then meticulously record the detail of my observations and, finally, I work out how to slot it all into place. I coast in neutral gear until my editorial decisions are made: what to keep, what to reject and what to change.

How have times changed in your field?

Bombsites were my playgrounds. As a child I remember standing amongst the rubble imagining it all back again. When I started studying architecture many buildings worth preserving were being demolished. Someone once explained the act to me as Britain's attempt to shrug off its regimented past; the symmetry of surrounding buildings symbolised unfashionable power and status. Parisians were painstakingly cleaning The Louvre whilst Londoners were tearing down past façades; it was the mood of that moment and it is not so now.

Your reputation is built upon a love of architecture. Which building fires your enthusiasm?

All buildings have a message to deliver but for me the pre-renaissance period represents England's most individual statement. I recognise splendid examples of England's contribution to our European heritage in parish churches and landscaped parks. For me, the parish church is more telling than the grand country house. Church architecture is a constant reminder that art history partners social history; some of the finest English sculpture can be admired in places as diverse as Westminster Abbey and parish churches in the country.

Does nature inspire you?

Yes, but principally for aesthetic and conservation reasons.

Do you believe that decoration should answer to architecture?

Yes, architecture is the greatest art and the two must work together. Decoration must respond to the building, yet everything I do requires someone to like it. I understand that balance and am cautious about the pitfalls.

How do British designers compare with their global counterparts?

Mediterranean-based civilisation has coloured my ways of seeing life. I have never ventured to the Far East. My visual understanding and life perceptions stem from England, Ireland, Morocco, France, Central Italy, Greece, Egypt and beyond to America. The French and Italians may be grander but the British are more inventive and daring, their ways of seeing are more ingenious. Conran followed in the footsteps of William Morris: he tidied up English taste and influenced far afield by opening Habitat. Whilst his peers presented with more sophistication, he delivered the goods. If I had been more cerebral about my approach, I would have tried for the starkest like John Pawson. But being married with children makes minimalism a difficult route! Anyway, my youth was spent during the sixties. It was a decorative, colourful, relaxed and very freeing time and so it was not possible in my mind to think the minimalist way.

How do you measure cultural style?

The best barometer is on the streets. It starts in adolescence; our young, especially our art students, demonstrate an edge on the rest of the world. A depth of appreciation for more complex aesthetic detail grows later on. Art students and artists self-express best; it is the way they cut their hair, paint their faces, pierce their bodies, pose, set out and live in their homes.

Conserving the past or building the future – what matters most to you?

Both. In conservation, it's vital not to freeze over. It is important to thaw out and be flexible. Everything must change; preserving any building is a temporary solution that fits a moment and a given need. But every future strategy must understand its past in order to move on. I think England struggled architecturally after the war partly because it couldn't digest the bulk of its heritage. English Heritage provides real meaning by going back to the roots and setting clear rules and regulations. Sometimes a building worth keeping comes up and you can feel that its heart has gone but its purpose and meaning remain relevant. The Royal Opera House is an historic building that serves a specific function that people of today want and value. Decoration-wise, I recognised its previous integrity and saw something worth keeping. But the space inside was totally deconstructed and put back with a new interior map and better services. Sometimes it is harder to repeat a scheme of decoration than to start from scratch.

Are you inspired by contemporary design and do you find it fitting for our built future?

Yes, there is clear understanding, confidence and vision. Design has become a global phenomenon for better or worse. There are new conquering symbols to replace the Union Jack and Lipton teas. Retail interiors and hotels are the ones to watch. The Calvin Klein store in New York is a strong statement that influences nearly all of its Madison Avenue neighbours. It is the same with hotels; look at I.M. PEI's Four Season interiors in New York and Philippe Starck's new hotel rooms in London.

Why are the two projects you selected to feature in this profile sentimentally special to you?

Beningbrough Hall in Yorkshire, where I worked for The National Trust, is special because I was allowed to keep it simple; we didn't install display lighting or stay to arrange the cushions. Spencer House is appreciated a great deal and London is my city. Interestingly enough, it took seven years to restore and seven years to originally construct back in the 18th-century. Lord Rothschild, the client, understands everything.

Do most of your clients understand you and your work?

Not always, but some are very perceptive. One once remarked, 'You don't want anything I've got, David, do you?' And that was true. I don't. For me, appreciation has nothing to do with ownership; admiring does not mean possessing. I have never understood stealing for that reason.

What do you expect from a client?

Let me read you this morning's fax from Lord Rothschild concerning a staircase in a house in St James's Place. "Beauty in my book is more important than comfort, so if scale and incline are respectively smaller than normal, so be it." Patience and empathy also help.

How do you sign off from each job?

I never sign off from a client or a project; my door always remains open.

Over the past 20 years, English Heritage has taken steps towards protecting cinemas: in 1981, there were only 17 listed cinemas in London; today there are 43. English Heritage intends to list some more and is currently holding public consultations before seeking government approval for their plans. Do you think that giving such cinemas the opportunity to apply for restoration grants represents architectural progress?

Yes. In conservation terms, London's old cinemas are impressive and unusual structures. Before television, when the moving image still inspired wonder and awe, cinemas were built as shrines to glamour and fantasy. A trip to the pictures resembled a brief sojourn into a dream-like other world, a great escape from everything mundane and familiar. It would be interesting to recreate one of the old atmospheric cinemas I recall from my youth, when a night at the pictures was accessible and affordable yet a true flight of fancy. The last time I visited the new six-screen Virgin cinema in Fulham Road I tried to map it out as it was, from my memory. I spent ages pacing the aisles and searching the Gents for the original column bases. It was originally called the Forum and the interior details were borrowed from Ancient Rome; very good it was too.

What's next for you?

I think my best work is still to come because I am increasingly fascinated by the challenges new projects bring. As long as I am not standing in young talent's way, I intend to carry on working for as long as I am asked to work. Perhaps one day that sponge will be dry and all squeezed out, so it will need to be dipped into something else to regain its moisture. If that happens, I will hang up my hat and perhaps study something in a completely different field.

DESIGN REDISCOVERY

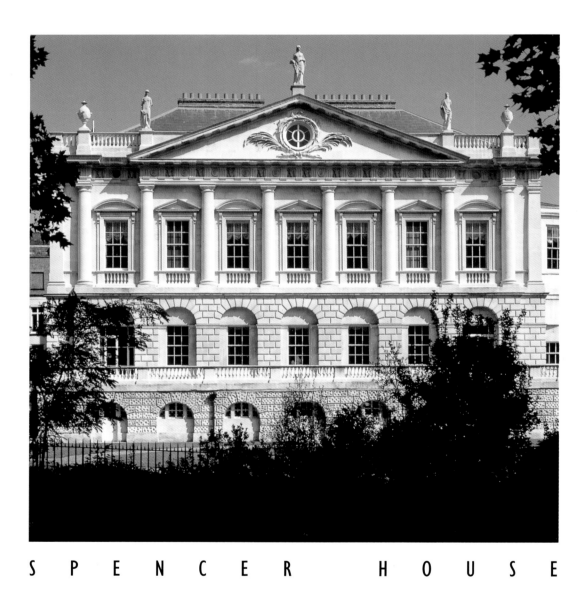

S P E N C E R   H O U S E

DAVID MLINARIC

DAVID MLINARIC

DESIGN REDISCOVERY

B E N I N G B R O U G H   H A L L

DAVID MLINARIC

DESIGN REDISCOVERY

DESIGN REDISCOVERY

JANE CHURCHILL

JANE CHURCHILL

Jane Churchill and decoration, Silver Cross and prams, strawberries and cream, Wimbledon and tennis; familiar words that conjure up images of Britain's aristocratic past. Jane Churchill's world of decoration is historically blue but the former wife of Winston Churchill's cousin prefers to labour hard rather than live life as 'Lady Charles'. She entered the design arena as a teenager and started her first retail outlet at the age of 21. During the eighties, she built her decorating business up to six shops before selling Jane Churchill fabrics and wallpapers in 1989 to her original employer, Colefax & Fowler. The continued promotion of that core collection has made her name a lifestyle brand. Jane Churchill's own third millennium vision is still decoration and its mission is permanently grounded in her Pimlico retail roots. But she constantly ventures out into associated realms of the unknown. Her latest design project concerns a tired British icon and a familiar mobile home.

What's on your mind?

Prams and Baby Fairs. But perhaps it should be wheelchairs and Help the Aged housing!

Do you like what you see?

Certainly not the sickly greens and bright yellow colour schemes that are part of the contemporary pram world. There are some interesting new accessories on the market that serve an extra lifestyle need for modern parents, like the pram Land Rover has created for joggers. Silver Cross's concern is fundamentally the same as ever, getting babies and toddlers reliably around from A to B in comfort, safety and style.

Silver Cross Prams, the ring of it all sounds a bit lost and unloved – aren't they best left to a bygone era?

It is true that the name Silver Cross was salvaged out of receivership. But I am working as a consultant on the design and promotional front for the new company. Silver Cross is an innovative and distinctive brand; the original concept has been revamped and creatively updated. Looking around, it is difficult to spot any real competition in its market. If Silver Cross can get it right there is a real chance to offer something unique to parents. People nowadays have families later, they have more disposable income and they see sense in investing in something well-crafted and original. We have upgraded the interiors with child-orientated fabrics, soft blue fabrics that tell nice stories about white rabbits and floppy ears and ABC letters. For me, this is a project that presents real opportunity and creative challenge.

Is it important for you to keep progressing in the sense of moving on?

I never want to stop and let the grass grow over me in life. I have always taken on new ventures because it stops me from churning out another chintz sofa.

Under your name you developed one of the earliest 'decoration' brands but then sold it. Any regrets when you look back and see your namesake now?

Not at all. I don't like it when things get so big that I lose control. I understand what I can and can't handle financially. Tackling some new creative challenge is what it is all about, just like when we were producing a series of television programmes on decorating for the Granada network.

What do you think about all the new DIY shows being screened?

'Changing Rooms' is ghastly. I wonder who wants to live in a room where the design is inspired by a box of chocolates? I don't think that the media have woken up to the reality that people today want to aspire to things. They are better educated, better read, better travelled and generally enjoy greater disposable income. Interiors don't have to be opulent to be well done. A lack of vision and the downmarket attitude of producers stifle possible inspiration. Those interior programmes we produced a few years ago had a clear creative angle and delivered an effective message. What is important is to point things out to people and show different approaches to the world of interiors: like our tour of New York interiors, when we covered everything from the loft to the grand house. The Americans tend to like looking up with their vision and the British look down. You can see it reflected in the soap culture difference: compare Dynasty with Coronation Street.

The new-found public interest in interiors offers the media an open channel of opportunity. But, ultimately, isn't every creative project budget driven?

Of course. I completely understand that priority. It would be hard to find someone more conscious of budgets than me. I have had to be dedicated to budgets all my life. What is important is identifying the areas to spend money and where to compromise. You need to know where to go to source things and what to look for when you get there. And ultimately you need to understand how to put it all together as one good and simple design.

How did you acquire that ability?

It would have been hopeless for me to resist the creative urge because we have so many design genes in my family. I was brought up to notice things and throughout my childhood we constantly discussed good taste in relation to everything from food to houses.

So what's next for Jane Churchill?

I am not up there in a tower looking down: I am down there foraging out anything I haven't done before! I have extraordinary energy – for me an admission of tiredness implies enormous personal failing.

DESIGN REDISCOVERY

S I L V E R   C R O S S

AMANDA ROSA

AMANDA ROSA

Amanda Rosa is not a designer who would want to be mistaken for a concept. Her understated presence suggests a marque that may be pedestrian, mundane or just plain ordinary. And Rosa's claim to be the least glamorous person she knows would have you believe that her projects are going to be boring and dull. Yet Rosa has almost single-handedly crafted innovation back into the heart of contemporary Scottish design. And when Rosa is not designing she is planning to conquer something new in development. If she is not leading her Glasgow-based team on a project, Amanda Rosa is partnering a property investment with peer visionaire and husband, Ken McCulloch. Commuting the world from a Monaco base, they work as a team driven by a combative give-take dynamic. Their passionate game is interiors and property and the friction of two creative minds throws off sparks of pure ingenuity. Rosa's recent design focus was the priceless interior of what was once described as 'the Eighth Wonder of the World', Gleneagles Hotel in Perthshire, Scotland.

When the resort opened in 1924, Gleneagles was described as 'a Riviera in the Highlands'. Today it is a world-famous hotel and golf resort icon. Did you find it easy to move such an establishment into the third millennium?

I believe that our design input was the first really controversial event to happen in Gleneagles. The hotel realised that it had to attract a younger, fresher audience. At first, they just wanted more decor and more style. When it came on to the second phase, they dared even more colour, even more Scottish power. Brief-wise, they wanted tradition but not tartan, they wanted texture with no chintz, they wanted wool, they wanted suede and they wanted silk.

Gleneagles is an integral part of high society's calendar: yachting at Cowes, polo at Deauville and golf at Gleneagles, a five-red-star hotel set in an 850 acre estate. Did the landscape influence your interior design?

Definitely. How could the inside begin to compete with what is happening outside? Simply looking out of a window down the Glens is an oil painting; you just want the interior atmosphere to be warm and cosy to complement the landscape mood. The setting at Gleneagles is so magnificent and the countryside is so beautiful, you don't have to say Scottish inside.

How does one stay fresh in the design business?

It is important to see as much as possible. Ken and I look at life together and design is our life. I appreciate the 'wow' factor and, in truth, not a lot stimulates me in the UK. We have travelled a lot to America; Dallas is absolutely charming and Las Vegas is very inspirational. A visit to a restaurant over there can be complete

theatre. I remember one where the interior pivots around a 40-foot glass wine tower that racks about 20,000 bottles. Clad in black leather and a harness, a very attractive woman climbs up to retrieve your wine selection for the evening!

Give me an example of how such memories can translate into real life interiors?

A few years ago, we stayed in a resort in the upper New York State called The Point. It's a favourite mountain destination for wealthy New Yorkers during the hot summer months and during the 1930s it was a home for the Rockerfeller family. We went out of season, during early January, and its image stays etched forever in my mind. The rustic surrounds were contrasted against powder snow and the attention to detail throughout was incredible. Not long after we returned, a small project in the Lakes came up called The Dove's Nest. We based its concept on The Point and crafted cabins in the grounds out of unused, old buildings. Material-wise, we went back to basics, using slate and stone, and the furniture was designed to look very old. Dove's Nest creates its own special magic. When Nicole Kidman and Tom Cruise were in London, they used it regularly because it is so very private; you can helicopter in and nobody knows you are there.

Do you use technology to change the way you approach business?

No. I have never lost a job yet because I am not wired up to a computer. For me it is all about touch and feel. There is no heart or soul in a CAD drawing. I find nothing to get excited about; whereas a technical drawing, done by hand, can be a work of art.

You are renowned for your strong use of colour. What makes your palette so distinctive?

I love colour, very plain colour and I work tonally; if it is blue then everything is blue. At Gleneagles, we applied muted Scottish colours from a setting of lavender, heather and fern. If there is any tartan, it is in a detail like a rug or a throw and even then it is more of a check or a mulberry than an ancient clan statement. I depend upon colour to create mood and feel. Effective lighting is also really important. The best interior in the world cannot communicate its drama without staged lighting.

What words are well associated with your name?

I am known for providing comfort with an edge. Perhaps I should claim to be a perfectionist but I am not. My designs are not the most striking around; they are simplistic rather than minimalistic. I like a bit of fun, something fairly inventive that ruffles a few feathers. That bit of extra spice in design makes the difference. Ken calls it the 'Oxo' touch.

AMANDA ROSA

G L E N E A G L E S

LET THE GREAT WORLD SPIN FOREVER
DOWN THE RINGING GROOVES OF CHANGE
— ALFRED LORD TENNYSON

JOURNEYS SHRINK OUR GREAT WORLD. CONCORDE AND SATELLITE JOIN OPPOSING HEMISPHERES LIKE SIAMESE TWINS. COSMOPOLITAN AND CONTRASTING IMAGES BEAM DOWN FROM OUTER SPACE INTO OUR LIVING ROOMS IN A MYRIAD OF NEW WAYS. CONTEMPORARY EVOLUTION MEANS OPENING OUT; THE ADOPTION OF NEW WAYS OF THINKING IMPORTED FROM FOREIGN PLACES. DESIGNER KELLY HOPPEN UNDERSTANDS THE GREAT CROSS-CULTURE BETWEEN THE EAST AND THE WEST, THE YIN AND THE YANG. LIKE A MASTER PILGRIM CROSSING BORDERS, HER PROGRESSIVE CRAFTING IS A NATURAL REACTION TO THE FUSION OF HOME AND AWAY. THERE IS NO GREATER MANIFESTATION OF CONTEMPORARY LIVING THAN INTERIOR DESIGN. IT IS A DAILY INVASION OF OUR OWN SPACE AND A MIRROR OF OUR SOUL. SO THANKS BE TO STAR PERFORMER KELLY: A LEADING LIGHT IN THE WORLD OF INTERIORS WHO IS UNAFRAID TO REACH OUT AND TOUCH A SWITCHED-ON AUDIENCE. HER MARQUE IS HIGH STREET AND HOPPEN ART MAKES HOT INTERIOR NEWS. SHE IS TO BE CONGRATULATED FOR HAVING WEANED A HUNGRY PUBLIC FROM THE COMFORTS OF BOTTLED INTERIORS ONTO A BALANCED, HIGH-FIBRE RICE DIET IMPORTED FROM UNFAMILIAR PADDY FIELDS. WE APPLAUD HER GENETICALLY UNMODIFIED ORDER THAT IS ORGANIC, PULPY AND LINEAR. HOPPEN WEAVES CONTRASTING LIFE FIBRES INTO ONE DECORATING LIFESTYLE AND HARMONISES CHINOISERIE INTO A SIMPLE YET EXOTIC SONG. PEOPLE EVERYWHERE HAVE GROWN TO RESPECT THE FACT THAT HOPPEN DIGS ROOT DEEP TO EXPOSE MORE THAN JUST HER LAST PROJECT'S GLOSSY PHOTOGRAPH. HOPPEN UNDERSTANDS THE COMMUNICATION NEEDED TO EXPLAIN AND NOT JUST PROMOTE HER EASTERN PROMISE; SEVERAL PUBLISHED BOOKS EXPLORE THE INFLUENCES AND INSPIRATIONS THAT LIE BEHIND HER STYLE. HER TEMPLATE BOOK, 'EAST MEETS WEST', INTRODUCED READERS TO SNAPSHOT MEMORIES FROM THE DIARY OF AN ASIAN GLOBE-TROTTER AT A TIME WHEN MOST SOUGHT COMFORT WITHIN THE FAMILIAR BOUNDARIES OF EUROPEAN HERITAGE.

J O U

n. the process of travelling from one place to another. The time taken or distance travelled on a journey.

KELLY HOPPEN

ADVANCED TECHNOLOGY BRINGS INSTANT RAPPORT BUT ONLY IN A TWO-DIMENSIONAL SENSE. WE MAY BE ABLE TO SEE AND HEAR WITHOUT EVER INTERACTING, EVER FEELING OR EVER TOUCHING. 'IN TOUCH', HOPPEN'S LATEST BOOK, IS A SOOTHING AND PROTECTIVE BALM FROM MODERN STRESS; AN ORGANIC OINTMENT BASED ON TWO INGREDIENTS, SENSE AND TEXTURE. IT EXPOSES THE LATENT CHEMISTRY OF THE WHOLE DESIGN PROCESS. TEXTURE IS THE NEW COLOUR THAT SEEKS TO PRISE OPEN TIGHT HANDS AND MINDS. HOPPEN INTERIORS ARE PRESENTED AS NATURE'S POWERFUL 'LIFE POSTURES'; THE GOAL IS TO ALERT PEOPLE'S INSTINCTS AND RAISE SENSORY POWER. IN THE FLESH KELLY HOPPEN IS A SPICY CONTRAST TO HER EASILY DIGESTIBLE TAUPE INTERIORS. A PALE-SKINNED BEAUTY WITH A CROWN OF APRICOT HAIR, SHE LOOKS MORE LIKE A PAINTING THAN A PERSON. THE PERSONALITY IS A CELTIC FIZZ AND IT COMES AS A RELIEF TO GLIMPSE HER LIGHTER SIDE BECAUSE OTHERWISE SHE WOULD BE TOO SERIOUS TO BE TRUE. LIKE AN ART STUDENT'S HEROINE STALKING ACROSS THE ROOM, STARING FIERCELY LIKE A FOX WITH GREY-GREEN EYES FIXED ON YOUR PERSONAL HORIZON, SHE DELIVERS HER DESIGN BELIEFS. HOPPEN BELIEVES THAT MODERN FAST-LANE LIFE GENERATES A NEED TO BECOME MORE BASIC. WE MUST CREATE LIFESTYLE ENVIRONMENTS THAT ENCOMPASS FEELINGS LIKE SENSITIVITY, SERENITY, REJUVENATION, BALANCE AND INTUITION. PART OF HER MAGICAL DESIGN TRIP RAISES UNFAMILIAR VOCABULARY LIKE 'SHAMANIC ENERGY'. FOR HOPPEN, MOVING ON IS WHAT THE LIVING HOME IS ABOUT AND HER MARQUE ALWAYS INCLUDES GREEN ORGANIC LIFE. AFTER OUR PROFILE INTERVIEW I FEEL I OUGHT TO CLAP, FEELING SOMEHOW BLESSED YET ALSO FAINTLY DISTURBED. THIS ACTIVIST DESIGNER IS AS RESPONSIVE TO THE AESTHETIC DESIRES OF CLIENTS AS SHE IS TO THE NEEDS OF THE EARTH. SHE KNOWS HOW TO SEW NEW SEEDS AND BRANCH BUSINESS ROOTS OUT INTO VIRGIN SOIL. THE BRAND APPEAL IS WHOLESOME, FRESHLY SQUEEZED AND PITHY. HOPPEN CULTURE USES A 'TOUCHY-FEELY' PLATFORM TO PUSH HER LABEL AND SEW IT INTO THE MINDS OF MILLIONS. KELLY HOPPEN BRANDED LIFESTYLE IS TOTALLY 'IN TOUCH' WITH THE FUTURE WORLD OF INTERIORS.

R   N   E   Y

Vb to make a journey. (Old French *journée* a day, a day's travelling).

KELLY HOPPEN

SEEDS OF CHANGE

SEEDS OF CHANGE

TODAY'S VIRTUAL DESIGNER IS WELL CONNECTED. HE PREDICTS A BILLION GLOBAL 'CLIENTS' BEFORE 2010. (SIZE MATTERS WHEN YOU'RE AN ICON 17CM TALL WITH AN IMPLAUSIBLY LARGE HEAD AND AN IMPLANTED SMILE). HE NEVER STANDS ANYONE UP. HE DOESN'T DO BAD HAIR DAYS. AN IMMACULATE CONCEPTION, HE APPEARS AT A RESOLUTION OF 360 DOTS PER INCH. BE PREPARED. THIS DESIGNER IS DESTINED TO BEAM INTO YOUR LIFE VIA THE INTERNET. 'VIRTUAL' IS A PIONEER: A SORT OF ALTERNATIVE DESIGNER 'CHEAP FREAK' WHO IS INTO CAD AND INSTANT SOLUTIONS. HE IS PROGRAMMED TO LEAD US THROUGH OUR SCREENS INTO A TWO-DIMENSIONAL WORLD, DEMYSTIFYING THE WAYS OF ALTERNATIVE INTERIORS. SINCE WE NOW HAVE THE POWER, HE IS A 'SILLY NOT TO' LIFESTYLE INVENTION. ONLY DIE-HARD CYNICS RECOGNISE HIM TO BE OF 'MILLENNIUM DOME MENTALITY'. A NEW GREENWHICH TERM FOR AN ARCHITECTURAL DISORDER WHERE SUFFERERS FEEL COMPELLED TO CONSTRUCT TECHNICAL MONUMENTS TO SATISFY A HYPOTHETICAL AUDIENCE NEED. THANKFULLY VIRTUAL DESIGNERS PROCTER AND RIHL'S HOLOGRAPHIC SKILLS DO NOT EXTEND TO INTERVIEWS. THE REAL, FLESH-AND-BLOOD CHRISTOPHER AND FERNANDO TURN UP AS ARCHITECTS TO TALK PASSIONATELY ON A ONE-TO-ONE BASIS. BUT ON THE PHONE, ON THE NET, ON E-MAIL, ON CAD, THE DUO HERALD TECHNOLOGY AS THE ULTIMATE SOLUTION. THEY DON'T BELIEVE THAT AS WE WIRE THE UNIVERSE, WE SHORT-CIRCUIT THE SOUL. THEY LIKE THE FACT THAT INDIVIDUALS, WHEREVER THEY ARE, CAN CONNECT. AND, WHEREVER THEY ARE, INDIVIDUALS ARE CONNECTED. IN FACT, THE GREATEST FEAR OF DIGITAL LIFESTYLE PROFESSIONALS LIKE PROCTER AND RIHL IS THE SOUND OF SILENCE. ONCE UPON A TIME, ARTISANS WERE SELF-CONFESSED 'TECHNOPHOBES': INDIVIDUAL ISLANDS WHO NEEDED TO GET LONELY TO FUNCTION. 'NIL BY MOUSE' GREAT DESIGNERS OF THE PAST REFUSED TO BITE OFF ANY MORE THAN THEY COULD CREATIVELY CHEW. THEY TAUGHT US TO BELIEVE THAT IN ORDER TO SPIT ART BACK OUT FOR THE REST OF US TO DIGEST THEY NEEDED SPACE. THE OLD FERMENTING PROCESS REQUIRED TIME AND PRIVACY. AT THE TOUCH OF A BUTTON NEW TECHNOLOGY HAS THROWN OUT THE RULES. NEW WAVE DESIGNERS LIKE CHRISTOPHER PROCTER AND FERNANDO RIHL TRUMPET THAT CHANGE.

T E C H N

n. the application of practical or mechanical sciences to industry

CHRISTOPHER PROCTER   FERNANDO RIHL

'TECHNOLOGY INSPIRES US' EXPLAINS PROCTER. 'NEW TECHNOLOGY ALLOWS US TO MAKE THE GRADE BY LOOKING AT LOTS OF DIFFERENT IDEAS AND COMPRESSING THEM INTO REALITY. MOST OF THE COMPLEX SHAPES FOUND IN OUR ARCHITECTURE, INTERIORS AND PRODUCT DESIGN COME FROM COMPUTER MODELLING.' THE ARCHITECTURAL PARTNERS ARE INSPIRED BY EVOLUTIONARY FRONTIER DESTINATIONS LIKE TOKYO AND PRAGUE. THE PROCTER RIHL COLLECTION INCLUDES 'FLOW SHELVING' CRAFTED FROM BIRCH PLY, 'WEB TABLES' FROM ACRYLIC AND STAINLESS STEEL, 'SYNAPSE VASES' AND 'SPACE LILY BOWLS' MOULDED FROM ACRYLIC. 'THE JAPANESE DEMONSTRATE AMAZING DESIGNS AND AMAZING AESTHETICS. TOKYO AS A CITY MAY WELL REPRESENT A REALISTIC FUTURE SOLUTION FOR OUR CROWDED WORLD. IT IS SO ALIEN, SO CHAOTIC, SO FICTIONAL YET SO TRADITIONAL'. THROUGH THE EYES OF PROCTER RIHL, THE JUXTAPOSITION OF CHAOS AND TRANQUILLITY TRANSLATES INTO AN ADMIRABLE 'CARTOON-LIKE' STYLE OF MODERNISM. THE RESULTANT ARCHITECTURE DEMONSTRATES NEW SENSIBILITIES TO GUIDE A FRESH APPROACH TO GRAPHICS, CERAMICS AND LANDSCAPE DESIGN. CHRISTOPHER AND FERNANDO SIMULTANEOUSLY COMMEND CZECHOSLOVAKIAN ARCHITECTURE SET IN THE CONTEXT OF A TRADITIONAL EUROPEAN CITY. THEY PROFESSIONALLY APPLAUD THE DISTORTED SHAPE OF BUILDINGS MADE POSSIBLE BY COMPUTER-GENERATED GRIDS. THEY BORROW THE STAID, CLEAN, STARK MINIMALISM OF CZECH 20S AND 30S CUBISM AND STAMP ITS CRYSTALLISED FORM ONTO THEIR PERSONALISED CRAFTING. PROCTER RIHL'S UNIQUE ARCHITECTURAL SIGNATURE APPEALS TO PRIVATE CLIENTS AND FELLOW ARTISANS ALIKE. FASHION DESIGNERS AND LANDSCAPERS ARE PARTICULARLY IMPRESSED BY THE PARTNERSHIP'S STRUCTURAL KNOWLEDGE OF HOW TO PUT NEW MATERIALS TOGETHER. ADMIRERS SAY THEIR INNOVATIVE APPROACH CREATES 'TECHNOLOGICALLY ADVANCED AND AESTHETICALLY PLEASING' TRANSPARENT PIECES: EACH SIMPLY CRAFTED FROM GLASS, PERSPEX OR ACRYLIC. PROCTER RIHL'S SCULPTURES HAVE COMPLEMENTED LONDON'S FINEST CATWALK COLLECTIONS AND GOLD MEDAL WINNER 'GARDENS SANS FRONTIÈRES' AT CHELSEA FLOWER SHOW 2000. THE WAY PROCTER AND RIHL SEE IT, SUCH DIVERSE 'FUN' PROJECT EXPERIENCES LET THEM ABSORB DIFFERENT DESIGN APPROACHES IN PLACES FAR REMOVED FROM THE DAILY CONSTRAINTS OF BUILT ARCHITECTURE.

O L O G Y

or commerce. Scientific methods or devices used in a particular field.

Architects Fernando Rihl and Christopher Procter's virtual solutions assisted garden designer Ryl Nowell to win a Gold Medal for 'Gardens sans Frontières' at Chelsea Flower Show 2000. The theme for the garden is based on a remark made by Lewis Carroll's Alice that the countryside is 'marked out like a chess board'. By shifting the formal perspective grid created for the garden's principal structure, Procter and Rihl effectively focus attention on the plant blocks. Transparent sculptural glass and steel structures were designed and constructed to float above the strongly coloured beds set with cabbages and other unexpected plants. Procter and Rihl's surreal reflections: people, sky and plants set in a theatre of glass diamond pavilions and a glass bridge over rippling water. 'Gardens sans Frontiéres' represents the juxtaposition of a virtual dynamic with simple geometry and mother nature.

G   R

SEEDS OF CHANGE

LONDON-BASED AGENDA 21 ARCHITECTS PRACTICE AS ENVIRONMENTAL SPONGES NOT SPONGERS. PROFESSIONALLY ENGAGED IN A MISSION TO ADDRESS THE CHALLENGES OF THE THIRD MILLENNIUM, THEY BUCK THE ENDURING SUSTAINABILITY OF NON-SUSTAINABLE ARCHITECTS. THEY DELIVER TECHNICAL AND ARTISTIC EXCELLENCE. THEY BUZZ AROUND WITH AN ARCHITECTURAL STING IN THEIR DESIGN TAIL THAT IS A NATURAL SELF-PRESERVATION INSTINCT. AN UNPOLLUTED REACTIONARY FORMULA DEVELOPED FROM THE DRIVING SPIRIT OF THE EARTH SUMMIT CONFERENCE HELD IN RIO DE JANEIRIO IN 1992. HANDS ON GREEN HEARTS, NARINDER ASSI, TARSEM FLORA, JAMES GROUX AND GEORGE PETRIDES ARE AGENDA 21 ARCHITECTS. THEY OFFER OVER 100 YEARS OF EXPERIENCE. THEIR APPROACH IS PART OF A CONTINUING COMMITMENT TO INTRODUCE NEW AND INNOVATIVE DESIGNS THAT ARE ENVIRONMENTALLY AND SOCIALLY RESPONSIBLE AS WELL AS TECHNICALLY SUPERIOR. THE GOAL IS THE CREATION OF BEAUTIFUL DESIGNS FOR PEOPLE TO ENJOY. AGENDA 21 WORK WITH THE SPIRIT OF ARCHITECTURAL INNOVATION AND SEEK TO SOW THE SEEDS OF CHANGE. THE 1992 UN EARTH SUMMIT'S AGENDA 21 ACTION PLAN EXPOSED A BRAND NEW STYLE OF ART: A PAINTING THAT BLENDS WORDS LIKE CREATION AND DESTRUCTION, EQUILIBRIUM, NATURAL BALANCE, ECO-SYSTEMS, SUSTAINABILITY, BIO-DIVERSITY, INTERDEPENDENCE AND SPATIAL INTER-RELATIONSHIPS. AGENDA 21 LINKS MAN'S BUILT ENVIRONMENT WITH A BIGGER FULL-LENGTH FEATURE. IT STARS THOSE UNIQUE ELEMENTS: AIR, MOTHER EARTH, WATER, FIRE AND AETHER. NONE OF US MAY EXPERIENCE THE EARTH'S INEVITABLE CONCLUSION BUT WE ARE EXPOSED TO THE DAILY EFFECTS; THE LONGER HOTTER SUMMERS AND SHORTER MILDER WINTERS. THESE PROFESSIONAL CRAFTSMEN DESERVE PUBLIC ACCLAIM FOR CREATING THEIR AGENDA 21 AND BREEDING AN ECO-REVOLUTION THAT RESPECTS NATURE.

adj. a colour between yellow and blue; the colour of grass.

TODAY, WE LIVE AND BREATHE DESIGN. FEW URBAN AND RURAL EXPERIENCES - AT HOME, AT WORK, AT LEISURE - ARE FREE FROM ITS MIDAS TOUCH. WE HAVE ABSORBED DESIGN SO DEEPLY INTO OURSELVES THAT WE NO LONGER RECOGNISE THE MYRIAD WAYS IN WHICH IT PROMPTS, CAJOLES, DISTURBS, INFLUENCES MOOD AND EXCITES US. IT'S A NATURAL GIVEN MAN-MADE NECESSITY. IT'S JUST THE WAY THINGS ARE. EVERY ARCHITECTURAL DESIGN IS AN ENVIRONMENTAL COMPROMISE. EFFECTIVE DESIGN ICONS UNDERSTAND THIS POWER OF SEDUCTION: A BUILDING'S EXTERIOR AND INTERIOR IMAGE. THIS IMAGE REACHES US FIRST AS A VISUAL ENTITY - PERIOD, SHAPE, COLOUR, FORM, TYPE, FUNCTION AND STYLE. BUT IF IT IS TO WORK, ITS TOTAL EFFECT ON US MUST BECOME AN IDEA THAT IS VISUALLY AND KINAESTHETICALLY APPEALING TO EACH OF OUR SENSORY PERCEPTIONS AND THE MOOD OF THE MOMENT. IT NEEDS TO LOOK AND FEEL RIGHT. AT HOME WE CREATE OUR OWN MINI-WORLD, OUR PERSONAL SANCTUARY IS A MICROCOSM OF THE BIGGER OUTSIDE WORLD. IT'S EASY TO LOSE SIGHT OF OUR LINKS WITH OUR WIDER HOME: THE PLANET ITSELF. QUALITY DESIGN AFFECTS US ALL; GOOD DESIGNS ENRICH INDIVIDUAL LIVES, ENCOURAGE CIVIC PRIDE AND BREATHE NEW LIFE INTO URBAN SPACE. WE NEED TO KEEP ON ASKING 'IN WHOSE INTEREST AND TO WHAT ENDS?' EVEN IN OUR MANMADE CULTURE — WITH ALL ITS BLIND-SPOTS, DISTORTIONS, PRESSURES, TRENDS, OBSESSIONS AND CRAZINESS — IT REMAINS POSSIBLE FOR DESIGNERS TO PRESENT AND PROPOSE ALTERNATIVE WAYS. SIMPLY BY SHARING WITH US A GREEN VISION AND PROVIDING A FORMULA FOR OUR DIGNIFIED SURVIVAL AND CO-EXISTENCE: BY INSTINCTIVELY BUILDING WHAT COMES NATURALLY. AT ROOT, IT'S ABOUT CHOICE AND RESPONSIBILITY. WE OWE THAT DUTY OF CARE TO THE WORLD'S FUTURE GENERATIONS AND OURSELVES.

E   E   N

A person who supports environmentalist issues: used in a political context: green issues. (Old English grène).

SEEDS OF CHANGE

Agenda 21 Architects are Narinder Assi, Tarsem Flora, James Groux and George Petrides. Together they paint the built landscape green again with aesthetic and sensory crafted pieces. They lead us on our way back to our roots. Back to a primitive way of handling earth engineering. Inspired by organic forms and materials. It is the moment to be close to nature. It is time to be close to the earth.

Nicholas Haslam is a legend sometimes known as society's decorator. The anti-hero of his time, Haslam has almost single-handedly broadened the mystique of interior design to an international symbol of style and class. Wherever he goes - his media name goes everywhere with anybody who is somebody - Haslam infuses his own image as a symbol of youth, excitement and rebellion.

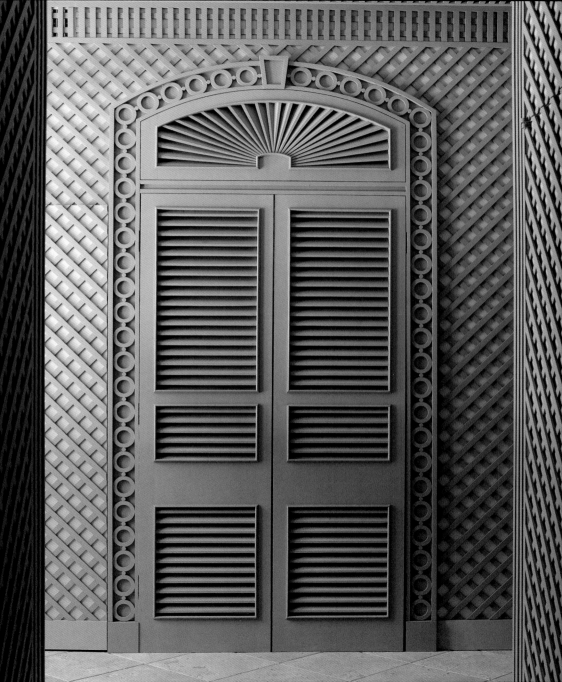

Is there a time for chintz and flora, a time for being bare; is there a time for high street shopping, to find the right interior to wear ? Is there a time for tying ribbons, a time for fur and skin; is there a time for laying tables, a time for thick and thin ? Here he comes, heads turn around; here he comes, to take his crown. Is there a time to run for cover, a time to kiss and tell; is there a time for different colours, different taupes you find hard to spell? Is there a time for looking back, a time for east meets west; is there a time to turn to feng shui, is there a time to copy the best ? Here he comes, image plays the tune; here he comes, surreal in his crown.

Fantasies

JOHN HACKNEY   DAVE WATERS

This is the Body Zone at the UK's Millennium Dome. You've come through the elbow. There's no going back now. You're about to laugh, cry or scream. What's coming next? That depends on how you like your entertainment. You hear a heart beating. Its rhythm consumes all sense of time. There it is: hanging huge, bright red and pumping. Must you go up? There's a blood-curdling scream.... Suddenly, it's all over. Or perhaps it's just begun? badoom, badoom, badoom....

from the heart

FANTASY

Roll up, roll up. Roller coaster through your body. Experience the emotions of your life. Scream your scariest scream. Laugh your loudest laugh. Cry yourself a river. Run sperm race 2000. Journey up your elbow to be repulsed by skin and bone. Step inside your skull for a bit of a joke. Gaze though the lens of the world's largest eyeball as your emotions run dry. Sense your heart pumping pure adrenaline through your veins. Roll up. Roll up. This is the body for everybody.

JOHN HACKNEY   DAVE WATERS

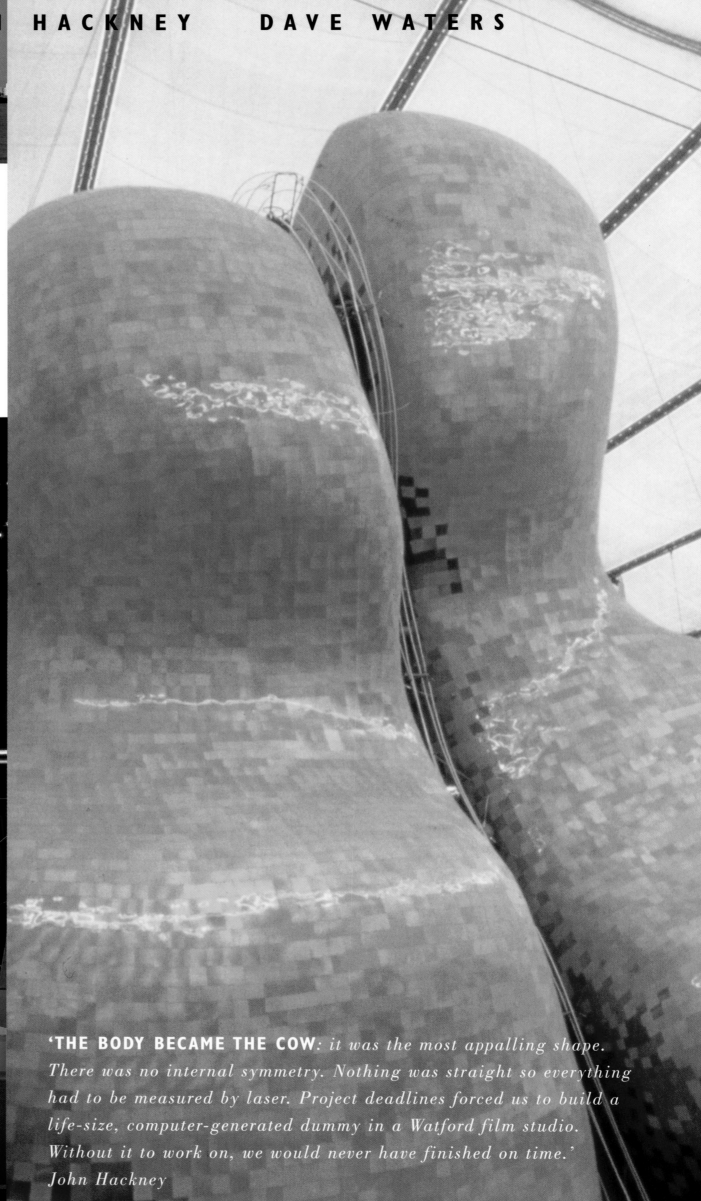

The millennium celebrations demanded an iconic structure. The Dome is a response to a 300-acre site, a climate and a timescale. Like a big top umbrella, it was erected to protect visitors from wind, rain and sun. Structurally completed within one year: its roof stands 50 metres high with a circumference of 1km. The Dome's project priorities were exterior matters: architecture and landscape design. Its interior content and the likely use of the site after the millennium experience were never this big top's priority. Revered as the main attraction, the Body Zone's creative team had just five months to design and fit out its guts and mortar.

FANTASY

'**THE BODY BECAME THE COW**: *it was the most appalling shape. There was no internal symmetry. Nothing was straight so everything had to be measured by laser. Project deadlines forced us to build a life-size, computer-generated dummy in a Watford film studio. Without it to work on, we would never have finished on time.'*
John Hackney

JOHN HACKNEY   DAVE WATERS

The Body Zone's creative brief was entertainment driven. The team, under the direction of John Hackney and Dave Waters, embraced emotive themes set to one central script. 'It was predicted 12 million people would walk through the Dome. Our job was to entertain a cross section of humanity rather than a target audience. We constantly rejected anything too abstract, too high brow and too intellectual. We wanted a Body for everybody', explained Hackney. The interior had a unique deadline: 5 months construction time. 'Nothing like the Dome had ever been built before and it promised "everything" gift wrapped up into one show. In the beginning, I think we were expected to come down and somehow sprinkle fairy dust over the proposals.' For Waters 'the currency of having no time' made the project an incredible experience. 'The Body was the ultimate no-holds barred brief and we directed it with pure tabloid instinct: we hit the ground running. In our familiar world of advertising, we make 90-second snapshots of entertainment. Editing is what we do. We approached the Body project like a film: it had a movie-type budget and a movie-type feel.'

Acutely green, everything put into the Body had to be bio-degradable and return to its organic roots when the final curtain falls in 2001. Under Hackney and Waters' co-direction, the Body used state-of-the-art technology and sophisticated themes to expose a segmented vision of the human emotional zone. Its script followed a roller coaster route designed to trigger raw feeling. Each set was represented in its own space. The soul, the muscle of each 'arena', lies dependent on the talent of its given apparatus. Each visitor entered their own emotional theatre: imagination made the Body experience a very personal drama. Travelling through, there were no subtitles: since the creators believed that word guides tend to imprison human perception. The entrance via the heart room was spectacularly scary. A giant heart was suspended on the loaded horizon. Its pulsating presence generated fear and apprehension. What happens next? Time for a laugh inside your own skull. Comedian Tommy Cooper played the brain, visually recognisable by his trademark red fez. He spouted forth the best edited minutes of Body jokes, 'Just-like-that'.

FANTASY

'**THERE'S NO STOPPING THE SPERM RACE 2000.** *The runners take off, they launch and they dance an aggressive dance. The screen seems to come right at you as the invaders try to score a life or death goal.*'
Dave Waters

JOHN HACKNEY   DAVE WATERS

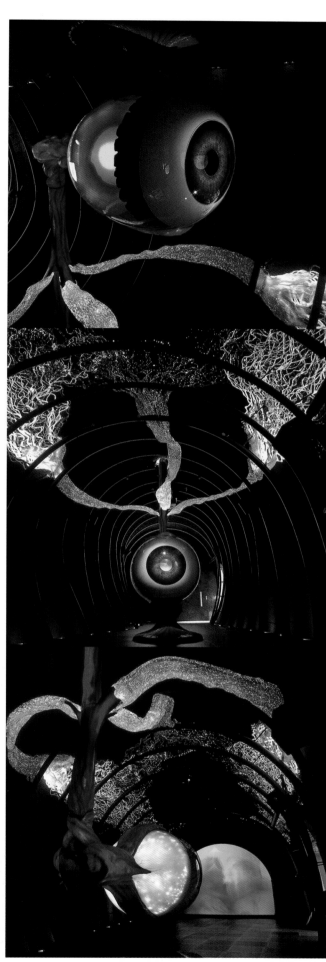

The sense of revulsion was explored in the 'Skin Room'. Lice skated over the cracked 'Sahara' surface and giant crabs popped up between pubic hairs to take some air. A giant pierced belly button stared down like an eye compelling your vision towards the 'bloody' abattoir floor. Human reproduction was celebrated in a giant 'womb room'. Cartoon sperm attacked an egg to an African drumbeat played by a septuagenarian with 38 children. Scores of computer-generated tadpoles war danced through a sperm race 2000. 'We wanted to create a fun space', said Waters, 'So we ran a multitude of layers of projection onto a circular overhead screen 18ft wide and the sperm charge at the viewer from above in a vast cathedral type space. Creatively we became 100% reliant on the content of the film and its drum beat rhythm.'

Entering the 'Eye Ball' theatre was a beautiful experience. Brilliant fibre optics created the surrealistic mood. A rich tapestry of naked life footage projected onto giant screens; the effect stimulated a sense of unsophisticated reality. Random scenes fused into one poignant performance that reached out to make its audience cry. Coming out of The Body completed a once-in-a-lifetime ordeal. You would have projected yourself in this zone for a moment....but it appeared that eternity had been expressed. Journeying through severed bone and muscle was the final act. 'We wanted people to leave feeling an enormous sense of physical relief.'

FANTASY

Fantasies

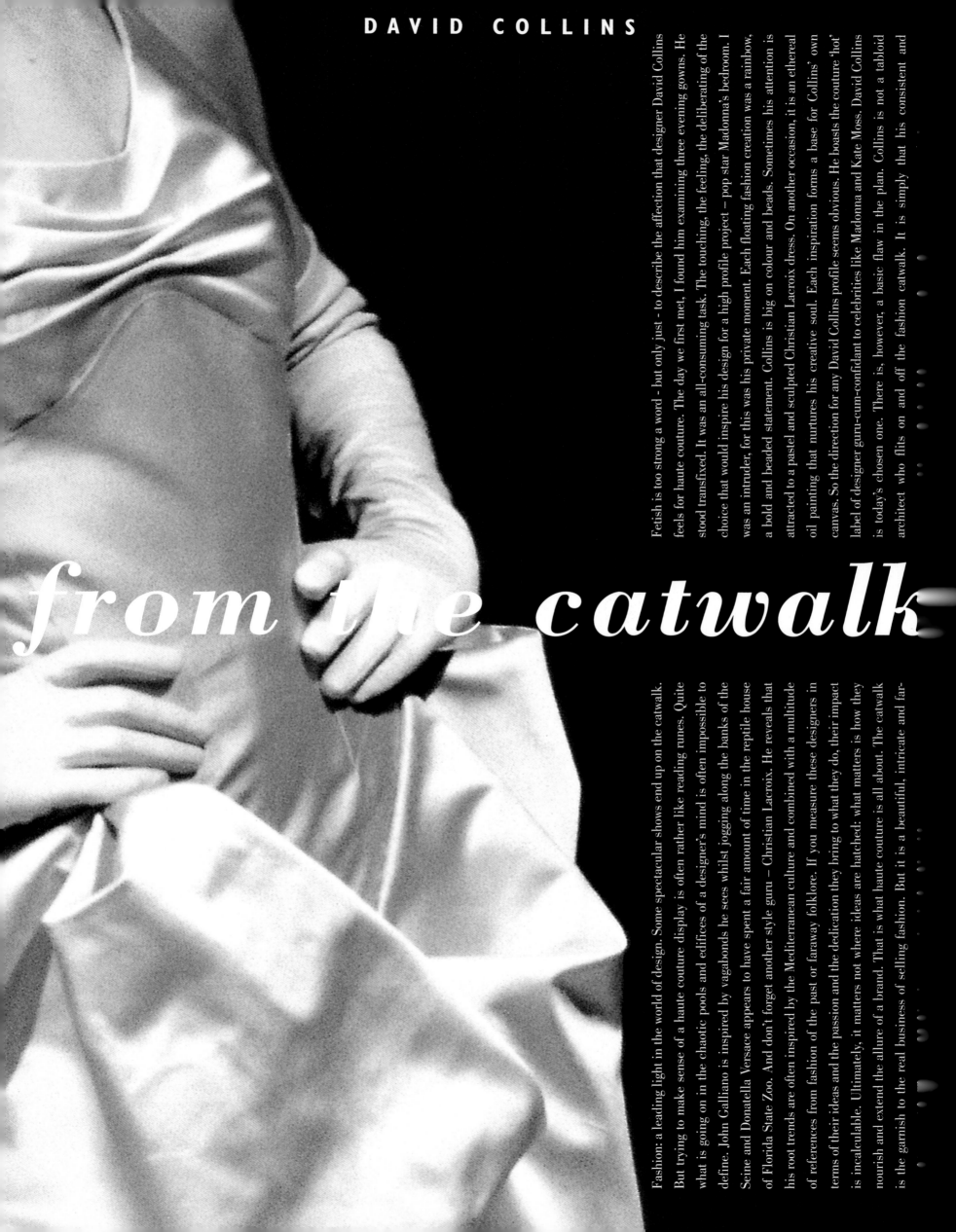

Fetish is too strong a word - but only just - to describe the affection that designer David Collins feels for haute couture. The day we first met, I found him examining three evening gowns. He stood transfixed. It was an all-consuming task. The touching, the feeling, the deliberating of the choice that would inspire his design for a high profile project – pop star Madonna's bedroom. I was an intruder, for this was his private moment. Each floating fashion creation was a rainbow, a bold and beaded statement. Collins is big on colour and beads. Sometimes his attention is attracted to a pastel and sculpted Christian Lacroix dress. On another occasion, it is an ethereal oil painting that nurtures his creative soul. Each inspiration forms a base for Collins' own canvas. So the direction for any David Collins profile seems obvious. He boasts the couture 'hot' label of designer guru-cum-confidant to celebrities like Madonna and Kate Moss. David Collins is today's chosen one. There is, however, a basic flaw in the plan. Collins is not a tabloid architect who flits on and off the fashion catwalk. It is simply that his consistent and

from the catwalk

Fashion: a leading light in the world of design. Some spectacular shows end up on the catwalk. But trying to make sense of a haute couture display is often rather like reading runes. Quite what is going on in the chaotic pools and edifices of a designer's mind is often impossible to define. John Galliano is inspired by vagabonds he sees whilst jogging along the banks of the Seine and Donatella Versace appears to have spent a fair amount of time in the reptile house of Florida State Zoo. And don't forget another style guru – Christian Lacroix. He reveals that his root trends are often inspired by the Mediterranean culture and combined with a multitude of reference's from fashion of the past or faraway folklore. If you measure these designers in terms of their ideas and the passion and the dedication they bring to what they do, their impact is incalculable. Ultimately, it matters not where ideas are hatched: what matters is how they nourish and extend the allure of a brand. That is what haute couture is all about. The catwalk is the garnish to the real business of selling fashion. But it is a beautiful, intricate and far-

FANTASY

DAVID COLLINS

An Interview

David Collins is an architect who is passionately interested in decorative detail and design finishes. For him, it's all about objects of desire, impulse and attraction. Collins is a man with innovative design ideas that set off a chemical reaction. He is a practical Modernist and an inventor with an eye for lifestyle scenarios. His recent high profile restaurant commissions include London's Mirabelle, J Sheekey's and Quo Vadis. But although Collins' current cachet may relate to his client Madonna, the man across the table from me in his Canary Wharf Office is not a material man or celebrity sponger. David Collins' priority is perfecting and building his expanding portfolio. He comes across as being generous-hearted, direct and loyal to his instincts: he is eminently likeable. Collins' work often appears serious, severe, determined and architecturally dogmatic. However, like the personality himself, the spaces he evokes are personable, joyful, reflective and, on occasions, they state what you might not expect to hear.

What's on your creative mind?
My creative mind is always focusing and looking. I am constantly trying to think of new things. In this business, the challenge is balancing the conflict between the creative side and the practical side. To deal with that, I have learned to think laterally throughout the design process.

Architect, interior designer, space planner, furniture designer, decorator, artisan etc – what tag best describes David Collins today?
I think of myself as a designer. I trained in Dublin as an architect and so my starting stance is architectural. What follows on after that is simple embellishment and sex appeal.

Do you find that architects generally find it difficult to interpret an interior in the sense of thinking full interior picture?
Yes, particularly in America. Americans tend to find an architect and then a decorator. Our design approach follows right through to the last detail.

Why have you chosen to open an office in New York?
To service a need and because a lot of our portfolio is based there. At the moment we are in a glamour cycle and people associate me with glamour.

And are you happy with the perception?
Yes, although glamour is a term that in my own mind relates to fashion not architecture. But glamour is an exciting and alluring point of reference that extends even to minimalism and I enjoy being like a chameleon.

What originally drew you into the field of design?
I wanted to work in a flexible environment. I wanted to find something creative that had integrity and stretched beyond the nine-to-five framework. In architecture and design we have professional parameters and obvious constraints.

Did you enjoy any particular childhood passions like drawing?
I was useless at drawing. But, like learning to ride a bicycle or learning to swim, with patience and practice you pick it up.

What are you passionate about?
Reading. I am a voracious reader. I devour everything and anything, fiction to non-fiction.

Is it possible for you to walk into a room and not rearrange the setting?
Absolutely.

In your experience, are creative skills instinctive or learned?
To an extent they are instinctive but I watch people in my office learn them as I learned them. My design psyche is transient – I instinctively understand that my role is to emulate other people's taste.

Is it true that you have a short attention span?
Yes. But in the sense that I don't like wasting time. I also don't like the process of analysis and I don't like analytical people. Design is about stimulating an emotional response and reaction. Design is best interpreted on a creative and emotional level. I don't believe that design stands up to analysis. That is why I find it difficult to talk about my design. You either respond to it or you don't respond to it. It either works or it doesn't work. It is either valid or invalid. You either like or not.

Do you direct the design of every project that comes on board?
I am very much involved at the conceptual stage and if key elements start to change I step back in and get involved. We increasingly identify areas that overlap between projects. For example, the introduction of innovative finishes that suit our designs. I try to explain my ideas to the team and depend on them to find ways of interpreting that direction.

Do you believe in brainstorming?
Definitely. I don't rely on myself for the generation of new ideas. Most successful businesses that progress depend upon internal brainstorming.

Do you find that your current project mix of about 80% commercial and 20% residential provides a healthy working balance?
Yes, but it's not static. I like to have private clients because the scope of work allows me to develop innovative design ideas particularly in terms of finishes. Commercial clients often do not have the time or the money to commit to prototyping in the same way.

DAVID COLLINS

Do you see your business growing any bigger than the current size of 30?
That depends on the project portfolio and the team in place to manage it. I cannot compromise on the design integrity of our work. I enjoy the new ideas others bring. The point of design is the communication of an idea.

Tell me about how you communicate with your clients?
I get on well with clients and develop a good relationship with them. It is a two-way process that produces its own synergy. Clients get frustrated by designers when things take too long and designers get frustrated by indecisive clients who are constantly changing their mind.

Are you decisive by nature?
No. I taught myself to become decisive. It is a business discipline rather than an innate part of my personality. My creative energy encourages me to remain open and keep the blinkers off. If I change my mind ten times it is because my mind is not closed off from what's going on around me.

Has your name always been associated with leather, beads and detail?
No. I find myself constantly adding to my creative vocabulary. At the moment, we are really intrigued by lacquer as a finish, so I used it in the 'Madonna bedroom' we designed recently.

What about the travel, do you enjoy it?
At the moment, travel means finding the shortest distance between A to B to get the job done. I don't like wasting time. The best thing about constant travel is the deadline discipline it enforces. Sometimes when I travel for pleasure I am inspired by the experience.

So where would you go for inspiration if you could?
Lots of different places. Paris is always inspiring for everything.

Do you ever go to the fashion shows there?
I am not in the fashion business so I don't go to fashion shows. To be honest I find them boring. I noticed and was inspired by the Christian Lacroix dress when it appeared in the magazine *Vogue* ages ago.

I understand you are a linguist. What languages do you speak?
Spanish, Italian and French.

Do you go to France a lot?
I used to, but now London is a bit more creative, so I don't feel the same need to go to Paris.

You obviously enjoy being in London?
Yeah. But I love Dublin and I get back as often as I can.

Do you welcome advances in new technology?
Technology is a very important part of new interior design. Technology fashions more and more shapes and places that we live in and it has simplified the whole design process.

Is the environment important?
In this office, we generally possess a subliminal awareness of the environment. For example, we don't use endangered materials. The architectural side of our work forces us to consider quite stringent regulations.

What is your own favourite architectural period?
I always think the present is interesting – no matter when the present is. I always go and look at new additions like the Dome and Tate Modern.

So which buildings in London do you architecturally admire?
I like different buildings. I like the Savoy Hotel for some reasons. I like Claridges Hotel for other reasons. I like the Eurostar tunnel. And I like some of the museums and banks.

Do you have any predictions for yourself 3-5 years on?
No. I have very little interest in anything but the present.

What makes David Collins different?
I don't care what other people are doing.

Do you care about what your clients think?
Yes, but I am not really influenced by that. People ask me more and more. 'David Collins – how come you are suddenly so ubiquitous?' But I have been doing the same thing for years and years. When you have the body of work that I have, then people are impressed by it.

Is J Sheekey's your favourite project?
Yes. I like it because of the attention to detail. It was modelled like a Chinese puzzle and I managed to make myself creatively invisible in J Sheekey's.

Was that important?
Yes. That is something that the British architect David Chipperfield achieves fantastically well.

Anyone else you particularly admire on the business front?
I admire lots of people. I am probably not that aware of many other interior designers because I don't really think of myself as being in interior design.

Who might you ask to design your own home?
I might ask John Pawson or Anouska Hempel.

FANTASY

DAVID COLLINS

In person, David Collins cuts a dash. His form is imposing, his gestures deliberate, his conversation sparse and I guess there are people who become totally unnerved in his presence. For David Collins is grand. He emanates the suppressed impatience of one who does not suffer fools at all, let alone gladly. Collins is the kind of creative perfectionist who is constantly disappointed when others cannot deliver his own golden standards. In conversation, if his appraising eye homes in upon a stray thread or misplaced object, it returns there time and again, distressed. Everyone who comes within his orbit instinctively knows that he has a particular abhorrence for undisciplined thinking. The David Collins mystique is born of architectural discipline. Collins is made of inner steel; he is an individual who doesn't swim with the current. One of the meatier design icons - he takes charge of everything from the architecture to curtain detail - Collins displays all the hallmarks of a true visionary. His crafted spaces boast architectural power and resonance. Collins' design work is a play on intellectual improvisation punctuated by bursts of joyous sensuality.

PEOPLE ASK ME MORE AND MORE *'David Collins - how come you are suddenly so ubiquitous?' But I have been doing the same thing for years and years. When you have the body of work that I have, then people are impressed.*
David Collins

FANTASY

Fantasies

from *afar*

Travellers bringing goods back from foreign lands have always influenced the development of their native cultures; we see it reflected in lifestyle disciplines ranging from art to architecture, from fashion to cuisine. 'This photograph means a lot to me, it is a record of something extraordinary and touching,' Tricia Guild explains and towns she has visited often become symbolic destinations. The favourites are ones that celebrate artisan traditions, value preservation, are beautiful for walking and kindle her desire to both consume and reflect. For Tricia Guild, the mission of travel is an exercise in seeing: learning how to document what moved her and figuring out how to bring the experience back home. Travel provides the opportunity to collect beauty and inspiration and weave these elements into a contemporary lifestyle. Tricia Guild appreciates the opportunity to fuse the ethnic heritage of one cultural background with another; her designs are as much linked to the cultural as to the natural. A trip might result in little more than the allure of the extraordinary scent of a flower or a memory of an ocean's particular shade of green. All of these documents, major and minor, set the 'Designers Guild' stage for Tricia Guild's evolving mosaic.

Rainbows are rediscovered in the saturated colours of an Indian wedding procession in Ranakpur. To experience that captivating feeling of being taken over, body, mind and soul by another culture is totally invigorating. Tricia Guild wanted to capture the romance of this moment: an immortal memory aesthetically conveyed by the colourful sensibilities of the sweeping crowd. Tricia Guild sees something quite extraordinary in India; she wants to interpret its magical quality and bring it into the contemporary homes of the West. India is a country of amazing paradox. Each region of the Indian subcontinent has its own distinct character and craft specialities. Every visit to India is a pilgrimage, a journey to the roots of ancient tradition and artistry. It is a country whirling in frantic street life, yet seeking peace and traditional stillness at its centre. India's enormous diversity reflects the colours of fire: the energy and heat of flame and its urgent sense of humanity. In India, one is never far from the artisan, for every person is ignited with an artisan spirit. The craft of hands in meditation or at work is a lasting legacy in this ancient and beautiful land.

TRICIA GUILD

Since its conception in 1970, Designers Guild has been telling the same story. The idea is simple: fabric, wallpaper and a beautiful starry summer vision. Designers Guild is a lifestyle dream in action, a space odyssey. Beautiful design creations that can be used in a very contemporary but informal way. Tricia Guild is constantly seeking out a concept within which people feel totally free to find what they are looking for, to develop their own fantasies. 'My whole world is about interior design and everything I do is about creating lifestyle. I have found a way of expressing myself that is inherently important to me. What interests me is encouraging people to enjoy accessing a stimulating and contemporary way of living. But, whilst Designers Guild style may be decorative, it is never nostalgic. 'We are not about recreating old documents or a look from a bygone era. My inspiration may originate from ancient textiles but I don't want to reproduce them. Designers Guild's goal is to develop its own modernity.'

Reflecting water. Water is our life source: tactile, flowing and nourishing. Water is all motion and depth. It is the most mysterious element, shrouded in an endless rhythm of solitude. It is vast, covering two-thirds of our planet and yet it remains as complete when isolated in miniature - a bead of dew, a raindrop. Water shows us the translucent colours of tranquillity and the deep shadow of ferocious strength and weight. There are many names for green to testify its obvious associations with nature. Each has a different effect on the eye, the imagination and the feelings. Different greens can be clean, calming, intriguing or inspiring to different people at different times. Green: synonymous with coolness, of lush atmosphere, of power and elegance. In colour there are no constants; no rules that can't be broken. A complete treatment for the stairwell in a home can carry a sense of style from one floor to another. A stairwell painted in a deep, saturated green can accentuate its form and play with the graphic design of wrought iron or architectural detail.

The brick walls are brushed pink and the ceiling is a dense clean blue stretching beyond like a high mesa sky. The bleached white starchiness running through the veins of the interior with its billowing glass panels suggests that you're in the Mediterranean, not London's Notting Hill Gate. Welcome to the house of Designers Guild. Breathe in the overlapping earth tone inspirations of its founder: Tricia Guild majors in natural light. At home and away, Tricia Guild surrounds herself with people and objects that invigorate. Like all creative souls, she understands that good energy thrives in positive environments and wants to transmit that power as an inspiration to others. 'I try to keep faithful to that feeling when you look at something and it comes together. You can feel it has something to say that excites you. Life is a constant search for something, like when an artist is painting and waiting for that moment. Design is about creating and perfecting that feeling or as much of it as possible'.

Objects: often placed like an afterthought in our homes yet the most constant source of daily inspiration and character. Furnishings we touch and feel are as critical as those elements used to embellish the aesthetics or sensory profiles of our 'nests'. Wood, glass, stone, metal and clay; forged, moulded, woven and carved into commodious shape by human hands, these raw materials marry form to function in everyday objects. We gather these materials into our space in the shape of furnishings because they offer a more sensual experience. That is why we invest in ceramic mixing bowls and wooden cutting boards instead of synthetics. Tricia Guild looks for objects inspired by the most honest of materials. Take a pure white egg: something very primitive and something very elegant. The egg is a creation, something that is loved before it exists. With natural elegance and cleanly moulded lines the humble egg transcends time; its familiar form comfortably delivers the feel of nature into contemporary lifestyle.

Tricia Guild may smile the shy smile of an eternal adolescent but she is quite clear about it. Tricia Guild's goal is to perfect her innate sense of modernity; Designers Guild's blooming business award for style directing remains a constant flame in today's world of interiors. Modern Master, Tricia Guild's brushstrokes have soul and set out to be challenging. And that is what makes her marque so intriguing.

ALL PINKS ARE SEXY AND ROMANTIC; *from the shocking pink of a Fifties evening gown to the elegant charm of a pale pink boudoir.*
Tricia Guild

FANTASY

Fantasies

NINA CAMPBELL

from the palette

Nina Campbell encourages us to rethink pink after its years of banishment. Pink has come out of the prawn up. It's hot to trot. Pink is absolutely ready to enter the world of interiors. Revamped and redesigned, it lends drama to interiors and a sweet innocence to the household stage. Nina Campbell explores its spectrum potential as a new basic that dramatically changes its mood with a change of textures. Powdery pinks have a place beyond grandma's bedroom door, while velvety pinks offer a theatrical style, conjuring images of the boudoir or the kissing couch. Glossy pinks are exotic and glamorous in an artificial way, recalling Hollywood perhaps, or a sculptural sixties interior. Pink's self-esteem is confident enough to wax lyrical and touch our sensual palette. Sink back into pink - it feels so soft and so good.

FANTASY

Stay for tea. Welcome home a familiar friend. Pink has gradually materialised back into our lives - a shirt here, a tie there. It's nesting in our closet, on the streets, and in our fashions. And now it's coming into our interiors. A wallpaper here, a fabric there. Perhaps it's pink's revenge to sneak in, intimately, easily, into our loaded lives. Once the debutante of a vivid colour range, pink gradually turned into a big softie. That 'elle' colour we didn't see or didn't want to see. But now the cycle has turned, prodigal pink is back, losing its associations with childishness and cloying femininity, and returning to its roots as an international colour full of passion and vibrancy. As the 'navy blue of India' pink is de-gendered and pervasive, as apt to show up on a soccer pitch as in the ballet class.

SEVENTY ONE

NINA CAMPBELL

Nina Campbell talks a lot on colour. Lecturing here, there and everywhere - particularly in America. The benefits of preaching to a wider audience led her to recently set up an office in Atlanta. 'In Kansas City I spoke to four hundred and fifty people. It raises a lot of money for charity and I am explaining my product my way'. Campbell presents her portfolio story around a palette base. She attempts to seduce people into not discounting colours. 'I start with orange. It always makes people gasp. Orange probably carries the biggest taboo mantle. Orange, to my generation, is a harsh sixties colour. Dead panic sets in at its mere mention. Yet nature demonstrates its individuality and potential so well. That's why I make my starting point 'sweet peas'. I try to get people to think about how to put it all together. Orange with terracotta, tangerine, apricot and wonderful soft greens, or silvery greys, yellows, and burnt sugars. Suddenly you begin to see orange. You have created a fabulous glowing interior canvas that is in no way harsh.'

Nina Campbell's business is a family affair: her daughter Henrietta manages the original shop in London SW3 and son Max tries to 'keep up' with his technology-orientated mother who is just about to fully embrace e-commerce. 'If you've been around for thirty years and you haven't moved on people are going to think 'Poor thing, she's still the same and she probably doesn't understand.' I believe in moving on and want to capitalise on the name we've worked hard to build.' Campbell's team creates two wallpaper and fabric collections each year which are distributed worldwide by Osborne & Little; she lectures and licenses many of her own products in Europe and the United States. Decorex 1998 saw the launch of Nina Campbell's range of carpets. Campbell's two shops retail her home accessories, gift ideas and a decorative antiques department called Nina bis. Nina Campbell has just completed an office in Moscow and a residence in Beirut. Her Parisian portfolio includes Le Parc, Victor Hugo and the Hotel de Vigny. And, together with David Linley, she redecorated the lobby of the Savoy Hotel in London.

NINA CAMPBELL

The evidence that Nina Campbell is globally inspired shines through in her Zanzibar collection of grand fabrics and 'trompe l'oeil' wallpapers. Similarly, the fragrance of France lingers over her Montpellier collection and the Chai Collection reflects her family association with the tea plantations of Darjeeling. One of her ancestors, Dr Alistair Campbell, was thought to be the first person to bring the tea plant from China to India in the 1830s. The prints are an eccentric mix of stitch and tapestry effects, exotic florals in tea-stained colourings, a summer pavilion trellis, even a large-scale thistle and a paisley check. 'I think you have to travel as a designer but that doesn't mean that just because you are fresh back from Morocco you insist on installing a tent for the next unsuspecting client. Nature provides real inspiration because she shows you how to combine colours that normally you wouldn't.'

'My mother wasn't very good about taking me to parks, so I grew up looking in wallpaper shops instead.' A protégée of Elsie de Wolfe, Nina Campbell's name stands globally as the epitome of English taste. She once won the American Fashion award for ' the woman who has most influenced style internationally'. Campbell trained under John Fowler, a mentor who in-bred in her the necessity to leave some project loose ends or escape routes. ' Not because I am incompetent but because at the end of every job you pick up on some extra spaces that would benefit from some extra spark. We have a first fit and then a second fit when we need the client to come along and make sure it's okay. For me it's a bit like cooking: you suddenly realise that you need a bit more salt, a bit more cayenne and in it goes. That does not mean we are not focused. As a company we pride ourselves on a personal, efficient service. We are focused on timing and budget and getting it done.'

Food is an interiors issue for Nina Campbell. The very edible magic of her paint collection is sparkle-dusted with 'think pink' names too sweet to ignore. Sugarcane, popcorn, butterscotch, toffee, olive oil, summer pudding, cassis, cranberry, raspberry are all on offer from à la carte Campbell. It's a tried and tested 'ring the bell' solution - a kind of Freudian flirting. For example, with brown she encourages people to 'trigger think' of chocolate, caramel and toast. Each word forms a delicious mouthful. Campbell tones her paints to match exactly with the wallpaper collections. The dramatically scaled design of leaves and pomegranates printed on heavy cotton chenille fabric spans five colour-ways and needs complementary paint partners.

Campbell's designs, like her Pomegranate Tree, have traditional roots but the fabrics are upbeat. The juxtaposition between design and nature appeals to her crafting and sometimes the integration of blue lends a modern touch to her prints. Blue is an ascending colour that spans its own spectrum yet mixes so well. Campbell recognises that texture, rich and inviting, is the happening thing in decoration today. The soft bloom of suede is incorporated into her recent collection because it looks friendly, lived-in, sumptuous and touchy-feely. Textured cotton is printed to resemble soft suede in a wide selection of plains and stripes. Campbell's palette of indigo, amethyst, charcoal, cream and gold happily receives newcomers like lagoon, denim and blueprint.

NINA CAMPBELL

In a quest for visual silence and peace at home many designers set a green interior stage. No contrast, no kitsch. Just an accumulation of green and green and green, all shades of green in an inventive array of tactile materials, from thick rush carpets to antique match-holders. Deep greens, sonorous greens, milky greens - we gather them, display them as proudly as we do photographs of family and friends. Greens on greens, solid or transparent, allow us to ground ourselves in a tradition linked with the organic world. In interior decoration, we increasingly mix modernistic and industrial designs with hand-made, unique and irregular products. Green hand-blown glass puts us in touch with organic materials in another way. Hand-made items of earth, sand and clay testify to human interaction with natural materials. Setting a green table is to set a new table - full of freshness, peacefulness and a touch of fantasy. It arouses the senses and stimulates the appetite, inviting us to eat.

Tall, angular white flowers. Only them. Lots of them. Caught up together in a vase. They are lovely. Deemed suitable by the literati as subjects for painting and poetry. A floral composition. The colour of flowers soothes us in the way looking into a green field or forest can fill us with calm. So we bring foliage inside our homes, to live with it, to be with it, to breathe it. We bring it in throughout our interiors because we need to offset a world where green is left behind in the rush to further technology. To look at beautiful, purifying flowers, cut down in their prime for our pleasure, is to look at the enigma of life and the cruel flux of time. Flowers are the symbol of the fragile and temporal nature of beauty. White lilies are the natural medium to show our own destiny. An impressive reminder to live our own lives to the fullest.

. . .

FANTASY

Fantasies from

'Rhythm in a garden is as important as it is in architecture. I see rhythm in the trees set in the distant horizon. I feel it when I'm planting hedges and flowers. I find it when I'm choosing colour. I love the rhythm of the seasons and the tranquillity of the autumn. I love the reflection found on water as the light touches it in different ways. I love the pitter-patter of the falling rain, that falls like music to my ears. Our lives are so full of noise, it takes concentration to hear the rhythm of leaves rustling and water lapping. Going to concerts gives me ideas about rhythm because I feel it in my music. And sensation, I like designing spaces which give sensations.'
Arabella Lennox-Boyd

a song of flowers

Plants and flowers, like babies, are brought up in nurseries. They need tender loving care, the right nourishment and lots of fresh air. Rhymes for the garden come as naturally for flowers as they do in the nursery for children. Pretty delicate blossoms seem to inspire poems. Or flowers become poems themselves. Little blooms create their own green writing, their own feelings. Garden displays give rise to pleasant emotions. They restore our affection, our fondness for simple and direct pleasures. Find the nursery rhyme written with Hellabores, their delicate colours and shapes sing little songs, which our eyes are made to hear. Take time to smell the flowers.

FANTASY

ARABELLA LENNOX-BOYD

An Interview

Impassioned with the rhythm of nature since childhood, Arabella Lennox-Boyd has been a landscape designer for almost thirty years. Her happiest years were spent growing up on the family farm north of Rome in a simple setting of timeless predictability: harvesting, olive picking and wine making. Today, as a new generation step out of their stylised interiors to discover that gardening is artistic, challenging and fun, they find Arabella Lennox-Boyd already out there, crafting the amazing. She is naturally committed to furthering the cause of contemporary garden design and has undertaken over 300 commissions, ranging from small town gardens to large, historical country landscapes. In her portfolio, there is a National Trust garden, a large roof garden, No 1 Poultry, in the city of London, and overseas projects from Bordeaux to Mexico, Germany to Canada and Barbados to the USA. She has also designed Gold medal-winning gardens for the Chelsea Flower Show, including a Best Garden Award in 1998.

Why do you do what you do?

I love putting my hands in soil whenever I garden. As a child I grew up understanding the countryside. The combination of a love of nature and a love of design brought me professionally into the garden. Because of the need to earn a living, I worked as well as studying landscape architecture.

What fascinates you?

Looking. I look constantly at the relationship between things. It is interesting to look when travelling at speed - on the motorway, on a plane or on a train.

What do you see?

On the motorway, for example, I like looking at trees; their height and their relationship to other trees. I compare the lighter Ash with the Oak. I look at the amount of shade they cast and what effect that has on the grass and landscape.

Is landscape gardening about relationships and space?

Yes. I believe that you shouldn't fill a space with trees but you should carve a space out of trees.

What are your particular passions?

Plants. I have been a Trustee of the Royal Botanical Kew Gardens for 9 years - as well as other landscape committees - and have planted thousands of trees and rare plants. I am also mad about long grass and meadows. It is fashionable now, but I have been doing it for a long time.

Do you like to leave a signature in your gardens?

No. If I did what I always wanted to do, it would always be the same! My work is not a signature, it is me trying to understand what is wanted by putting it into the proper scale and place and making it as wonderful as possible. I am there to give a client what they want.

Is it easy to understand what the client wants?

People don't always know what they want. It is important for me to like the client and the client has to like me. I have to interpret how they live and how they want the garden to relate to the house. Working with nature is a responsibility because you are dealing with something alive.

Nature does nothing useless, claimed Aristotle. How does one balance the taming of nature with the desire for presentation in the garden, order, harmony, identity and self-expression?

It is difficult! Sometimes I feel that it is better not to have a garden. Sometimes I feel - just give me a field with a view. At my home in Italy, we have a house with a view. Sometimes, I feel you want to stop trying to change the natural landscape. Human beings always want to interfere. Sometimes if you glimpse real beauty you should just leave it.

Does that present a challenge?

The challenge is to know when to let go. How little do you do, what do you leave? I remember a garden in Florence set on a hill with an amazing view. I puzzled 'How can I do a garden to interfere with that view?' In the end, I planted an evergreen structure all around the olive trees and in between them I planted fabulous white roses. They made a green and white frame but your eyes were still drawn to the drama of the view.

ARABELLA LENNOX-BOYD

Is there such a thing as a 'natural' garden?

No garden is totally natural. Even in most of the countryside, man has interfered. Maybe in Italy and France there are still places that belong to nature because man hasn't reached there.

Why are you interested in Japanese gardens?

Visiting Japanese gardens has provided total inspiration. The sophistication and the discipline of their design approach is humbling. In the West, we have too many ideas and we want to use all of them and perhaps they form a bit of a jumble. However, whilst I admire their discipline and search for perfection, I wouldn't necessarily want to recreate their ideas. Their culture is so different and their gardens relate to their culture.

Is a garden like a personality that you are building?

I suppose so. I try to understand the character, the spirit of the place and then enhance it. For example, if you have a shady place, I don't try to change that character. I will enhance or exaggerate it to give a deeper sense of shade, with the planting, the paving and whatever other tools I have at my disposal. I like surprises and contrasts. Designing a garden is a sensual thing.

How would you describe your approach to colour?

I am really interested in colour. I am amused by it. I am always experimenting with it. It depends on the garden I am in and the person who it is for. I prefer to be free with my ideas rather than be pinned down to anything.

Is that part of the attraction of Chelsea?

Yes. Chelsea allows me to be creative and approach something new. I always ask for a big garden and the ideas just come. Chelsea 2000 was my fifth.

Why is your own Lancashire garden such a well-renowned challenge?

Gresgarth Hall is my home and really the place I dream of. Sometimes, I feel that maybe it is over-designed because I try out my ideas and it has become a bit of a palette. What was so difficult was to combine what I see as important in a design, a certain amount of formality and simplicity, in a landscape that was very strong, very northern and very powerful.

Did it take long to complete?

It took me a long time. It just evolved. Being Italian and coming from a completely different environment and architectural background made it difficult. The house is Gothic in style and not something I was brought up to admire. I was born on the top of a hill and this house is on the bottom of a hill surrounded by woods and there is a powerful river running through the grounds. At times, the water is at peace and sometimes it becomes a raging torrent. I felt I had to go with the climate, geography and landscape. First, we cleared the evergreens because there were too many. Then we planted hedges that formed the structure of the garden and then many, many trees. Gradually the garden became like a cocoon around the house leading out into the landscape.

Is it the same learning curve for you in a hot climate like Barbados?

My first garden in Barbados was on a large site. When I started it was a vast crater in a derelict site set with beautiful Mahogany trees. I wasn't worried about not knowing the names of plants, but I felt I had to learn to get the tropical feel. I allowed myself a few days to immerse myself in the climate and vegetation. We went to see the public gardens and botanical gardens and travelled the island; the wonderful beaches, the palm trees, the water, the coral stones, and the rocks. I got to know the things I didn't like and the ones I did like.

Do you enjoy the researching and planning?

I love it. I try to live the design and imagine how my clients will use the garden. I don't mind doing a design and then redoing it and sometimes pulling it to pieces again. I analyse the site, put all the ideas and requirements together, and turn them into a coherent design.

What do you like doing best?

Everything. I adore everything about my job.

FANTASY

JOANNA WOOD

INSPIRATIONS

Joanna Wood set up as an interior designer in 1982. Her first business venture, Joanna Trading, started in Battersea and is now based in Pimlico Road, London. The Joanna brand comprises of five design-related companies: Joanna Trading (Interior Design) Ltd, Joanna Wood (Commercial) Ltd, Joanna Wood (The Shop) Ltd, Lewis & Wood (Fabric Company) and Larson Wood Ltd., an upholstery company.

Did you grow into design or was it love at first sight?

I tried a lot of things before deciding at the age of 22 that the only thing I really loved was architecture and design. Although I studied History of Art, I am probably now the least qualified person in my office. But that doesn't matter when you get to the top - my time is far too valuable to spend it drawing. It's one of those things, you need to know how to do it, but when you do know how to do it, you don't do it anymore.

What key words do you associate with residential design?

Quality, comfort, style and durability really matter but not necessarily in that order. Minimalism is an impractical reaction; a statement just like the chintzy, flowery 80s consumer society that also went too much one way. Real style and taste transcend fashion.

Do people rely upon designers to define and preserve 'good taste'?

It varies. Some clients are so richly educated in fine arts that they know more than the designers themselves, others are simply buying lifestyle and some have a dream and want you achieve it for them.

If taste is an individual thing why do we all have it?

Everybody has style. Taste is something completely different. Taste is in your fingertips, in your nose, in your eyelids. I have fantastically good people working with me and you can train it up to 95% to that last little drop, but then there is something in your bones that you are either born with or are not.

What are the tricks of your trade?

For an established designer, the most important thing is to approach clients like a psychologist because it is essential for you to understand how they live. One may have 4 kids and live-in staff. Another may be an outrageous gay from the south of France who wants to throw champagne parties every Thursday evening for 400 people!

Does the Joanna team believe in brainstorming?

Absolutely not. I don't sit round the table with my new juniors and say 'We have a manor house in Kent, what do you think?' We work together rather than brainstorm. The team here is sensational and my staff and clients tend to stay.

What attracts the clients to stay with you?

They get very looked after and loved and they appreciate our infrastructure. We don't screw up; we are on time, on budget and we produce what we say we are going to produce. Some of the great design geniuses, even David Hicks, went bust because of bad financial planning.

Is that because designers tend not to be budget-orientated?

Absolutely. We have a big team and I have two people working on accounts and a business advisor. I am not saying that my team is without problems. In the past we have been taken to the cleaners but it happens less and less and we are very efficient.

Is that why you segregated your areas of business?

I am very interested in all different facets of the business: I like designing furniture and wallpaper although it's a very competitive area and you have to produce something very different.

How do you split time to manage stuff?

I have a fantastic secretary who organises my diary because I am wildly optimistic. I always say something will be done by Friday night and then it is not acceptable to fail with that deadline. Reputation-wise we are known for having a source of talent but it is practical source. There is no point in committing to build a fairytale castle if you can't get the workmen, can't get the stone and don't know how the roof will be held up. We worry about the soap dish before we construct the bathroom.

Are people today more aware of the value of good residential design?

Definitely. I think Sir Terence Conran almost single-handedly changed the profile of the profession. He dragged design to the people, remains enormously creative and is still an incredible businessman.

What is changing your business?

Increased travel, new media and more leisure time have made a big difference. It has become a couture thing to know the names and the brands in lifestyle interiors. News-stands reflect the public interest with rows after rows of glossy magazines.

What are your passions?

Sir John Soane, because his architecture was classical yet totally innovative. And cashmere, which has become a current passion shared by clients because everything is becoming much more touchy-feely.

What do you never leave home without?

A tape measure. I might need to know how big the picture or moulding or sofa is and I always have my green folder with me - it is a constant reminder of those fifteen things I still need to do.

Jacqueline Nicolotti designs palaces for 'sultans of swing'. Back and forth, back and forth, Nicolotti commutes the London to Brunei trail. Her established list of Middle and Far Eastern clients includes the family of the Sultan of Brunei. The Sultan himself owns the world's largest residential palace. To give an idea of scale, Istana Nurul Iman in Bandar Seri Begawan in Brunei was completed in 1984 at a reported cost of £300 million: it has 1,788 rooms, 257 toilets and an underground garage housing 153 cars. Jacqueline Nicolotti's long-term business partner is architect Julian Harvey: he has devoted professional years to the construction of a £25M Scottish holiday home on the banks of Loch Ericht for a currency-dealer client. Constructed from imported granite, the 'farmhouse' boasts an underground ten-pin bowling alley, £3000 a-roll wallpaper and a glass-floored bar. Jacqueline Nicolotti's design judgement is not clouded by a gilded enthusiasm for carving a marque: her driving passion is contract negotiation and her philosophy is organisation and method.

What drew you into the Middle Eastern design arena?

My London-based architectural connections. One of our early projects was for the Sultan of Brunei's brother. I remember being given just 48 hours' notice to get organised and get out there.

Is it easy to interpret Middle Eastern taste?

The Middle East is not a single melting pot. It is impossible to compare a Saudi to an Arab. They are completely different: different approaches, different tastes, different countries and different requirements. It has been a tremendous learning curve working in the Middle East in terms of understanding cultures and observing protocol.

You have travelled around since childhood and fluently converse in four languages. What are your favourite cities?

Buenos Aires is wonderful. I spent most of my childhood there. It was designed in the 19th-century like a city with no expense spared: because it has never been bombed, rebuilt or grown organically, its architecture remains untouched by modernisation. Barcelona and Florence are also wonderfully put together and New York is a well-designed modern city with a logical grid and systems that work.

Do you maintain a design signature?

No, we are flexible. Decoration-wise we can do London minimum and we can do Baroque ecclesiastical.

If project style is a choice who makes key decisions?

That depends on the situation and we keep the blinkers off. For example, one current client favours a Japanese architect and so we instinctively follow that lead.

We don't impose our ideas onto clients: their home is their environment, it's their story to tell and taste to reflect. Clients with many houses dotted around the world present a special case. They can look to individual residences to project the enigmas of their personality or perhaps simply mirror each home's host country.

Does architectural style dictate the interior design?

We are always conscious that a building cannot sit on its own: it sits within a context and the whole context, including the external landscape, is relevant. In reality, there are priority considerations. For example, we have been asked to design the interior of an Islamic Bank with traditional architecture: the brief is for a modern interior, a complete contrast to the built exterior. Everyone understands that the Banking Hall design must be striking and simple.

Why have you maintained such a low profile in the UK?

Client confidentiality is crucial. In the past, because of the huge amount of work we did in Brunei, I made sure we kept our name out of the headlines. We have tried out new profile-raising ventures in the past but, for us, it is a difficult issue to address.

How was your reputation for providing hand-crafted furniture built?

Middle Eastern clients can traditionally afford to commission bespoke pieces: copies of museum pieces and old fabric documents rewoven from the past. It has given us tremendous satisfaction to help craftsmen stay employed by passing work on.

Is yesterday's craftsman threatened by extinction?

Unfortunately, yes. There used to be clusters of villages globally renowned for a particular skill, like Lyon in France: its trademark was fabric. The few left in the UK are kept very, very busy working on historic projects like the Opera House and the V&A museum.

What is the most difficult part of the job?

Not knowing what the client wants. Quite often, at the outset, we deal with intermediaries and have to prove our credentials to gain direct dialogue with the client.

Is trust important?

Doing what we do day in day out, trust needs to work on all sides. I am constantly amazed by the contrast of approach: some clients trust us from the start and for others it takes an eternity to get to that point.

If it's difficult to show client interiors, can you share your residential design philosophy as seen through the client's lens?

The Islamic translation attached to this artwork is perfect:
A man's home is his universe.

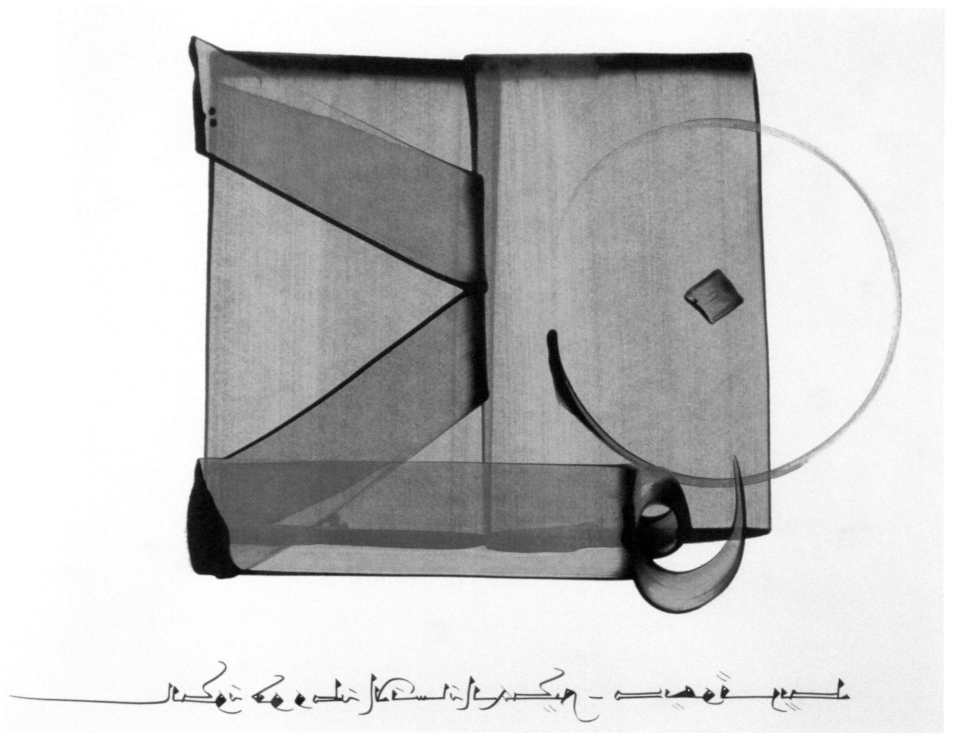

Anthony Collett and Andrzej Zarzycki tell a tale of integrity that for them needs no words. Their profile presentation is contained within a gravitas black linen box; it is a stoical recording of project life and a visual map of their wares. Meticulously constructed and classically clad, it illustrates their constant challenge to make something complex seem simple. The stuff of Collett and Zarzycki is of referential quality; it stems from a cerebral wit and an appreciation for all things tactile and sensual. The box shows image after image after image to reflect who they are. Each classic design is a complex crafted construction that relates more to architectural innovation than notions of interior decoration. Collett and Zarzycki explore the potential of space, matter and elements. They work their own thesis on a map of perfect symmetry and design with maximum impact.

Anthony Collett says on:

The job — Our focus is the top end of the residential market, the face of design. We are design led, we are into touching and feeling, the choosing of a colour, the creation of an atmosphere.

The Approach — For us it is not possible to separate architecture from its skin, which is our term for interior design. We like continuity and can offer all of the required skills. We know architects who work like architects and then hand over to a decorator who doesn't understand the detailing already in place.

Style — Our designs are born out of passion; they are eclectic and on the move. We have observed minimalism but don't follow that route. To us, you either are or are not - you can't sort of be a Jew. I once had a pre-occupation with arts and crafts and we enjoyed a mini ethnic fling but that is part of our internal evolution. If a Gothic project arrived tomorrow we would be excited.

The scene — Our job is over-glamorised and fundamentally more serious than the image portrayed. It is not about some nancy-boy waving a handkerchief around. If you take our professional cake and remove the design slice you leave a lot behind. Most of our time is spent making the thankless happen, dealing with contractors and resolving time and cost problems.

Communication — We appreciate how difficult it is for clients to link up with the right design crew to manage their project. We introduce ourselves properly during the initial courtship and like to clearly understand what makes clients tick. We provide lots of visual communication in the form of artistic impressions and perspective drawings to show the art of the possible. Taking new clients to finished projects also demonstrates the quality of what we are about.

Technology — There is that larger trend towards high technology in design. Because we operate CAD, we understand its benefits and the possibilities it brings. Sometimes it adds value, sometimes not. It takes time to do nice things

and technology may force quick decisions. For example, even receiving a fax suggests an instant reply and the predicament may deprive you of time to reflect upon a creative decision. Technology also generates furniture that is machine-made rather than the man-moulded crafted pieces we prefer.

The signature — A good project runs like a love affair; there is a lot of belief and desire. It is like a treat or a gift. We care and everything we do matters. Our most successful jobs evolve when we have crafted the architecture, the garden, the skin and the decoration. We understand the interface, how the inside and outside relate and pull together. Ultimately, the design becomes a transition, a complete look that doesn't appear whitewashed by one big brush.

Andrzej Zarzycki says on:

The partnership — During the creative phase, Tony and I work together 99% of the time on every project. We talk, we brainstorm and then progress it into a practical process. Sometimes, if I sail too close to a project, Tony comes in at 90 degrees to inject new life. That journey is a voyage and never a sea of conflict.

The Team — Somehow, fifteen is a manageable number and our lines of communication are clear. We view taking on new people as a serious business; it is like an apprenticeship. Our backgrounds are interiors-based but we have architects in the office. We are not overly impressed by bits of paper and credentials: sometimes they harbour mediocrity and prove meaningless. Some of our most skilled team members are not qualified architects.

Philosophy — One client had an old rustic French house that had been badly restored. It had a funny arch with a flat top and steel beam. To explain and convince the client what should be done, I produced a booklet showing my historic research and development of ideas from that basis, just for that one arch.

Innovation — Design innovation comes out of something else. You can't design in a vacuum. We draw on history and reference to remember and regurgitate things. Our vocabulary is quite limited; we are contemporary in style but our design route and its ethics are traditionally based.

Materials — In-house, our professional approach is personal, never impersonal. We like working with materials that involve people, technicians and craftsmen. We like stone and stone masonry. We like wood and will specially commission carved pieces. We like metal and forged metal work. We are not attracted to moulded plastic created by major machines.

Culture — Of course, everyone wants Vidal Sassoon to cut their hair. All our projects get tucked carefully under one of our wings for that reason. We have the dialogue with the client, we receive the brief, initiate the design work, expose our ideas and then rely on a very sound back-up to make it all happen.

ANTHONY COLLETT   ANDRZEJ ZARZYCKI

ANTHONY COLLETT   ANDRZEJ ZARZYCKI

 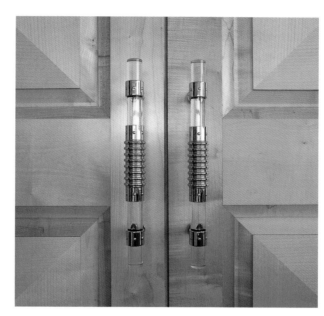 

WAYS OF SEEING

PHILIP HOOPER

Philip Hooper thinks architecturally. Hooper builds designs like cathedrals, every day drawing out the grid from which his creative drafts flow. The grid system fundamentally influences each manuscript of Hooper's craft and the designer's constant craving for structured drawing enables him to think a purely three-dimensional plot. Hooper depends heavily on his presentational skills and he leaves his graphics to do the artistic talking. Architecturally trained at Canterbury Art College, Philip Hooper is an enigmatic personality who is comfortable practising premier league design on both sides of the Atlantic: he has recently been project partnering with American designer, Sally Metcalf.

Philip Hooper says on:

Philip Hooper — My taste is catholic and I find my 'common sides' most appealing. Growing up in London and going onto building sites dressed up like some Vivienne Westwood pirate is part of that wackiness. I design listening to Led Zeppelin not Mozart and that rebelliousness affects my attitude towards things that come off my drawing board. I can't negate 'me' just because some people have some posh perception of how an interior designer works.

Project Partnering — Egos being as they are, it is difficult for top end designers to start doing projects together without some conflict. But Sally Metcalf and I manage the role well: we share the same pedigree and enjoy a symbiotic relationship. We work in catalytic fashion: constantly generating and developing our ideas. The huge advantage for me is that, being American, she doesn't share my pre-conceived ideas about suburban England. Together, we can take the looser American approach, one that isn't based on history and a past vocabulary that must be constantly recreated. Sometimes Sally will come at me from nowhere with a lime-green schizophrenic fabric and before I know it I am wondering if we ought to weave in some orange cowskin at the same time!

Designing in America — America is full of very wealthy families who want to indulge their interior fantasies. New money likes to acquire history and often people need to consolidate and express their elevated position in society. There is a French hamlet on the outskirts of Philadelphia which we are working on at the moment. It was constructed from salvaged materials imported from Southern Europe during the 20s. We have been given a 'footprint' of a small chateau and the challenge is to find and then deconstruct its original pomposity to ultimately make it more contemporary.

Understanding the rich — Most architects have no idea how rich people live. I do. When you have been invited to share weekends with people who are very, very rich you begin to understand their little quirks: how they work, how they play, how they live and how their staff surround them. In practice, that understanding of how to bring a home together.

Interior Design — Interior Design is not about buying off the shelf, it is about researching and re-interpreting and making something yourself. It is about not being content with being given a book: it is taking this and that and creating something new. Interior design is an expression of what you are about. People can't be taught interior design: individuals have to learn it in the field. You have to be skilled and instinctive and intuitive and able to do it without too much effort. You can't be blinkered or dismissive. You must be able to find something in anything. I always see something in everything; it is a creative sense that constantly drives me to interpret and recreate.

Design Theory — Interior designers today work in an editorial fashion by instructing artisans and craftsmen. I enjoy introducing some 'chaos' into a project by saying 'Okay you're twenty and mad. Go make me something and I will probably like it'.

Design labels — I can't have labels sewn onto me because I like to keep one-step-ahead. I want to be in a position to advance my design influence by being assertive enough to push ideas through. The goal is to create something that people sit up and notice.

The Fossil — I spotted the fossil pictured opposite in a marble yard. The stone-mason had carved away the marble leaving the fossil perfectly intact: it was a demonstration of his skill. Six years later, I bought it from him and set it behind a bath.

His observation deck — The Millennium Wheel is my favourite 'now' statement. It is ludicrous and celebratory and a real contribution to London's skyline. I don't care if it dwarfs the Houses of Parliament. Generally speaking, I find myself drawn to corners of, rather than whole, buildings. I particularly like the shrapnel-damaged corner of the V&A Museum, where Exhibition Road meets Cromwell Road. It presents as visible evidence that a famous urban building has seen conflict and survived potential destruction. Thinking that thought gives me goose pimples. People miss a lot by just not looking up.

PHILIP HOOPER

WAYS OF SEEING

MY IDEAS *are catholic; I enjoy jumping around different periods. Whether a skeleton says mid-century modern or 18th-century France, it gets the same amount of my detailing.*

MY INSPIRATION *is an empty space as much as anything else.*

John Solomon and Colin Duckworth just do it. They do absolutely everything associated with top quality residential design. Their happiest design moments are spent working with a laissez-faire client who is stationed overseas. One who leaves them, like beach-buoys stationed in a picture paradise set on distant shores, to play with proportions and space. Their goal? An alluring interior plan that can demonstrate their instinctive feel for presentation.

John Solomon says on:

The most memorable job — A huge residence in Kensington. The sheer logistics of achieving the project were challenging and everything very specified. We took full control and didn't see the client until it was all over.

Client communication — Client liaison is a major role. We wouldn't do a job for someone without the direct dialogue necessary to understand what the client was trying to set up. The chemistry must be right. It's a personality business.

Creative ideas — Clients want efficiency and style. In my experience that first idea is always the best. So when a client wants a selection you struggle to get the sixth because your sense of experience has drawn the best first.

Passions — Quality creates the ultimate satisfaction. Culturally, we say proportion, proportion, proportion like estate agents say location, location, location. Until you get proportion in a space, it can never be right. Classic Georgian property is always nice - you've got the proportion before you start - you don't have to go on to create it.

Time management — Our time is spent with administration, the rest of it is making sure you are on top of the builders. The creative bit takes very little of our time. Pacifying the client is also time consuming and happens because some things are simply out of our hands.

Budget matters — Before we start anything we cost out everything; we don't go beyond budget.

Colours — The decorative colours alter in accordance with client taste and given natural light. Middle Eastern clients are instinctively drawn to bright stronger mixes because their light is different from ours.

Personal taste — I studied Interior Design and Colin was trained in Furniture Design. We like natural materials and appreciate well-detailed joinery. We both come from that background. If we walk into a building that has no architrave in order to satisfy some minimalist design aesthetics, we don't admire it simply because we understand that it can't last!

Colin Duckworth says on:

The future — Minimalist most certainly not. Minimalist was clever in the beginning but people can't live like that. Clients don't want to perch on uncomfortable sofas in uncomfortable rooms. You have got to design what is right for the client; we don't impose our house-style on clients: we want to reflect and enhance their style.

Materials — Depend on the client/project need but must be in the right place at the right time. Personally I prefer stone to marble; most clients prefer marble, so I learn to like marble.

Client's style — For us , interpreting client style is a constant lesson in eclecticism and tolerance because, at the end of the day, our client is paying the bills. We're quite philosophical, rather than precious, about it. We don't impose a house-style on clients or put them in a box. If the client comes along and they want to have chintz, they get chintz; it will be nice chintz and look very smart.

Decorative budget options — We always give the client options; it's in the scheme of things to illustrate what they are. But you are trying to sell them something they can't perceive. If the client can't afford the best, it always shows to the detriment of the ultimate look, perhaps in the way the cheaper choice of curtains hang.

The project brief — One client arrived from Hong Kong; the only hint of a brief was the fact she liked Armani clothes. That was all we got. What she got was very slick; plain natural fabrics and plain colour schemes and we designed everything, including the furniture.

Client confidentiality — We don't give anything away beyond our four walls. Sometimes, we sign documents in respect of this assurance. Our clients are not interested in publicity; they have better things to do and don't need that kind of kick.

Inspirations — Plagiarism works well with us. Stealing not just from the past but from your knowledge. Stealing an idea from here and doing it there in a different way. The trick is knowing what goes with what and how to adapt things.

Global travel — Travel specifically for inspiration would be good, if we could afford the time; we don't go to Italy to wander round Rome each year. We're just normal people, who go to lie on a beach in Majorca for two weeks and soak in the sun.

JUSTIN MEATH BAKER

Three Globes as opening credits. The best entrance presents its own peculiar mystery. It lures you in. It begs that question. What lies behind? Why not guess?

At Harrington Hall, a Grade 1 historic mansion, we crafted a surprise cabinet bathroom like a jewel box out of a broom cupboard just 7 feet wide and 10 feet long. The last thing you'd expect to find hidden in the back of your wardrobe.

Converting a church hall into a surreal of glamour and theatre was this script: The Cobden Club Bar creates a new environment out of an 'institutionalised' cathedral-like space.

MARK HUMPHREY

Back to the future is more than a movie idea for designer Mark Humphrey. It is a way of revisiting, redefining and reclaiming the best from our past. Retro-fantasies. A fresh twist on a classic idea. The restoration of natural order: the past is de-constructed and bought back together as a simple and original composition. Humphrey lives and breathes design. His portfolio demonstrates innovative ideas for architectural interiors, space planning, furniture and accessories. Mark Humphrey is a designer striving to be somebody: if you really want to be somebody, you don't have to be great, you only have to be good. But good designers must live passionately by the golden rule – design surrounds us and begins from the ground up. It is under this driving philosophy, that the good among us become somebody to everybody. Mark Humphrey is good and destined to be somebody in the world of design.

MARK HUMPHREY

For me, says designer Mark Humphrey, drawings come easy.....words are more difficult. As an artist, Humphrey is a receptacle for emotions that come from all over the place: from the sky, from the earth, from a scrap of paper, from a passing shape, from a spider's web. His creative mind tries not to discriminate between things. Where things are concerned there are no class distinctions. His eye picks out from nature what is good and tries to translate it into contemporary lifestyle. Humphrey instinctively tailors everything: architecture, interiors, space planning, furniture and accessories. His portfolio of old drawings is his dictionary. Humphrey insists that his drawings are important for the artistic rendering of ideas because they have more immediacy. Even in childhood, Mark Humphrey's pencil drawings were full of precision and accuracy, expressiveness and vigour. Like notes in shorthand, they showed a marked ability to observe and simplify in a masterly way. But Humphrey is not interested in the forced naturalism of painstakingly accurate little pencil lines. Nor is he interested in the correct rendering of what he could see with his eyes. Mark Humphrey is interested in the reflexes that objects call forth in his own vivid imagination, and this is what he puts on paper with his pencil, charcoal, brush or even ink. It is in his sketch book that we are most likely to find clues as to Humphrey's design methods.

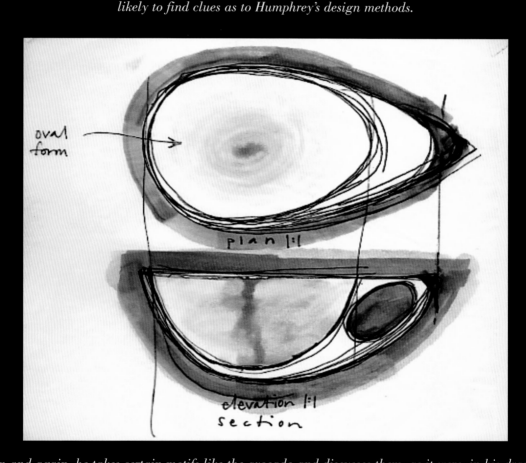

Again and again, he takes certain motifs like the avocado and discusses them, as it were, in his drawings, thus arriving at an endless number of new ways of expressing something, with only very slight differences between one drawing and the next. These are not meant to be improvements of an original draft, but a way of constantly and deliberately exploiting a particular theme. Humphrey doesn't aim for a final, conclusive formula for a motif. When we look at the different variations of a theme, they all form independent works of art. In relation to each other, they are like mirror images of the same object, but in the facets of a richly and elaborately cut crystal. You can see the immensely wide-range of his artistic expertise, his power of imagination and his ability to translate it into design practice. Humphrey is constantly making etchings, using a different number of techniques. He is forever searching for new methods to put his design ideas into practice. 'My creative angle follows the engineering behind the design rather than the architecture behind the design. If I don't understand how to put it together how can I instruct someone to make it? As a designer, I want to understand every integral part of the design world – from fashion to textiles, from graphics to landscape, from interiors to exteriors', he explains.

Malcolm Duffin upsets the menu. 'If you can't change, you can't design,' Duffin explains. 'As designers, we observe, we research, we connect and we journey in order to grow. We take a backward glance at Egypt to find form, order, maths and architecture. We turn to Europe for art and historic reference: to observe its cultural evolution. And for our next chapter, we look to America for precision, professionalism and a broad product range.' Duffin's Edinburgh-based practice is focused on raising new, reflective standards. 'We think that Scotland should build on its then heritage but not if that means ignoring now. Professionally speaking, we're not in the 'Dorothy does decorating set': we deliver a different design take. For Duffin that statement allows him to embrace minimalism: the art of making something look like nothing and making nothing look like something. And he sees signs that, after two hundred years of Georgian etiquette, some clients are making attempts to experiment with colour and modernity. 'One professional couple wanted to focus on light and create a gloriously unadorned space: they set about gutting the insides of a very traditional 30s house. And when they finally stood back to ponder just how to furnish this brand new testament of burnished beauty, we stepped on board delighted to help them clean it all up. So how does Duffin introduce his signature portfolio? 'In and out, shake it all about: we love those cheeky little jobs!'

CLAIRE NELSON

One designer and her dog: Claire Nelson and Brussel Sprout. Image matters and sometimes having a singular visual equity like Bruss provides instant recognition. But digging deeper into Claire Nelson's creative portfolio reveals some rather more objective measures to identify her distinctive performance. Part of a new generation of thirty-something designers, Nelson sets out in business to revive the professional scene. Not just by breathing fresh air into dusty old houses but by starting up a design studio on uncompromising terms. Nelson's ethos is hard work, and client empathy: she presents as a personable leader who instinctively defines her own parameters. A design graduate from 'Istituto Par L'Arte E Il Ristauro' in Florence, Claire Nelson's impressive portfolio bulges with restaurant and residential projects. Her up-beat design solutions draw on a panoply of references to make her finished interiors surprisingly eclectic. The integration of burnished wood, chrome, granite, glass and limestone into her work proves that it is possible to be grounded in tradition yet be forward thinking. 'I rely on textures like goatskin and mohair to create atmosphere and warmth and especially adore applying polished plaster finishes on walls.' To journey through her recently completed £3M penthouses at St James's Place is to recognise the collaboration of Claire Nelson's sensuous design statement.

DESIGN INNOVATION

DESIGN INNOVATION

DESIGN INNOVATION

Design briefs don't surprise Emily Todhunter and Kate Earle any more.

'We've created fantasy hotel suites. We've staged powerful rooms for escaping couples. We've been asked to set up interior backdrops that allow you to loose inhibitions, places to get lost in. One suite we designed was red hot, with Chinese moon-shaped openings, bamboo shutters, huge crimson silk drapes and an incredible bathroom panelled in oak. Another suite was frozen ice, cold and frosted with giant snowflake wallpaper. Because of the sexual connotation to the brief, we had immense fun brainstorming its artistic license. We spent ages planning where to put the dimmer switches!'

Todhunter and Earle talk fun but practise serious business. Some commercial projects, like Le Manoir aux Quat' Saisons in Oxfordshire for French chef patron Raymond Blanc, lend themselves towards escapism but most are residential with briefs firmly rooted in reality. 'We don't have big artistic egos to nurture. Design can be fantastically creative but it needs to get out there. Design has to be understood and it has to be bought. Design is not a performance art and it relies upon a sense of realism. We find the balance between home and theatre. We are passionate about colour, particularly weak colour: we love exploring the watery sides of beige. Our look is the softer side of modern and our vision is focused on the product side of interiors.'

Strong statements, like the product of their collaboration itself, and deliberately left open to interpretation. Emily Todhunter began her career as a specialist painter. Ask her today how to stay creatively fresh and the subject of paint always comes up. Her first interior design commission was a New York night club in 1988 and Kate Earle became a partner a decade later. It was that history that formed the friendship that formed the company that launched the Todhunter Earle products: wallpaper, fabrics and bespoke furniture.

DESIGN INNOVATION

A new romance. An old affair. You've spent reality years trying to forget. You've got the steady job, the mortgage, the children, the dog and the headache. You've settled down like your parents kept begging you to do. But sometimes that yearning for pure forgetfulness courses through your veins. Memories of an exhilarating sense of freedom dawn. You want to shut it out, shut yourselves in this Snow Queen fantasy suite. Your first love has turned up again unexpectedly, amazingly unattached and available. Share the laughter, feel the passion, skip a beat, re-live the first dance.

DESIGN INNOVATION

DESIGN INNOVATION

EMILY TODHUNTER   KATE EARLE

I HAVE NOTHING TO DECLARE

EXCEPT MY GENIUS

— OSCAR WILDE

GABHAN O'KEEFFE

When Sao Schlumberger wanted her portrait painted she commissioned Salvador Dali. She knew that Dali's provocative art reflected his obsession with what was forbidden in conventional society. Schlumberger had fantasised that the surrealist would transform her into the cat she once wanted to be. Instead, Dali froze Sao Schlumberger's image as a beautiful young woman in a green ball gown seated on a vast, flat desert, rays of light beaming down from the clouds onto her smiling face. The finished canvas lacked the vision Schlumberger craved. When Sao Schlumberger next wanted her portrait painted she commissioned Andy Warhol. She knew his medium was people. A brilliant self-publicist, Warhol was an enigma renowned for his artistic ability to demystify themes such as fame and death. Schlumberger's canvas was a perfect canvas for him to paint; versatile yet distinctive. Strong features that seem surprisingly easy to manipulate; sometimes making her a siren, sometimes a saint. Today Warhol's four portrait interpretations hang like mirrors on the yellow walls of the Parisian house that Schlumberger never leaves.

When Sao Schlumberger wanted her belle èpoque Parisian interior designed to reflect her colourful life story, she commissioned Gabhan O'Keeffe. She respected his knowing appreciation of make-up art and the part it can play in communicating an image. O'Keeffe portrait interiors are made for the fêted world that cultural icons inhabit - the lighting, the fantasy, the disguise and the make believe. Every Gabhan 'chez' is a naked reflection of a contemporary icon: larger than life figures who spin our great fantasy world.

GABHAN O'KEEFFE

The eyes of each Gabhan O'Keeffe interior stare out at you from the latest icon's stately home, challenging you to turn away. You can't. There is too much to see. O'Keeffe has skewered their seemingly unedited life in a fantasy of architecture, interior design and heavy design detail.

O'Keeffe designs tell tales that in the telling make a story. It is that story that makes the talk of the town. And Gabhan O'Keeffe enjoys making the music of his clients. He tunes into the cadence and rhythm of each personality to compose interiors full of their self-expression. Star-studded stars absolutely need star-studded interiors. Homes with expensive permutations that record all that's happening around them. A Gabhan canvas is complex and splendid; in your face and opulent. For O'Keeffe clients live life to extremes and have interiors set for their own theatrical life stage. Reluctant to talk about himself or his work, O'Keeffe rarely gives interviews. So my audience with the maestro proves more tempting than one with his internationally money-set clients, including Isabelle Goldsmith and Nan Kempner.

I expect him to be dapper, intense and a perfectionist: in person O'Keeffe is a likeable reality of that long inspired image. One-to-one conversation with Gabhan about the stuff of life is refreshingly simple and fun. What really matters to Gabhan is sharing the complexity of his craft and he sees me as his translator.

'No, no, no,' he says in exasperation when I ask to commence the recorded interview. He can't tell me anecdotes about his art before I have fully absorbed his portfolio.

'It's all instinct, completely instinctive, nothing is learned. For me it started with music around the age of four. There can be no better training. Life is about language and rhythm and how things interact and build up layer by layer.'

O'Keeffe recalls how his Irish grandfather bravely left his roots and heritage of traditions to start afresh in South Africa. And it was growing up in a land where 'everything just crawls' that Gabhan learned to gaze further and breathe deeper. He reveals a private album of photographic images that mirror silently through his crafting. The amazing colours, the vast skies, the wonderful bird-life and the adrenaline rush of meeting big game on foot has been forever etched on his mind. Look at his work and see his driving inspiration; the vibrant palette, brilliant beadwork, mixed-up prints and the brave adornments. A Gabhan room may be the season of light or a season of dark but it is always daring. Love them or hate them, O'Keeffe interiors are an inspiring sight for sore design eyes. Sheer and undiluted opulence, they reflect the best of times, not the worst of times. Intricate furniture, textiles and details all woven into reflective pearls of wisdom, each carefully strung onto a necklace that eventually becomes an interior.

'Look at this,' instructs O'Keeffe, his hands next pulling out some examples of the spin publicity that helps to propel his artistic image. He is particularly impressed by one recent profile review featured in a new American glossy and unimpressed that I haven't seen it.

There is another to examine; this time a hardback publication of his work. O'Keeffe nods in pleasure, enjoying the durability of its formal design whilst removing it gingerly from its sleeve. The theory of publicity is attractive to Gabhan but the visuals struggle to convey the meaning of his craft.

'I'm working with one and only one photographer at the moment. He totally understands my work,' he explains. Gabhan doesn't like crowds and is very particular about who surrounds him. But retaining a small 'comfort zone' team can prove difficult with some interior collections that require up to 35 individuals crafting on one detailed piece at a time.

Back to the portfolio library. Twelve volumes on, and the dreams and themes of Gabhan's clients are laid out in the interior souls of stars. Rooms like museum pieces that must house some of the world's best artwork.

'So you see, do you see?' asks O'Keeffe anxiously. 'You may think that my projects are going to be one thing and then it changes and then it changes again'. The maestro is playing to the tune of his client orchestra and it may be contemporary or upbeat, but the timing and delivery is perfection, an assault on all the senses of life.

An O'Keeffe interior is a collaboration between him, real life fantasy and the client; stars surrounded by trinkets that represent meaningful possessions. What comes out of that collaboration is alchemy.

We are sitting in a quiet, metallic room on the ground floor of a Belgravia mews studio. It is the birthing studio where his portrait interiors find life expression.

The office in which we are talking is small and dominated by Gabhan's huge desk, around which everything pivots: O'Keeffe doesn't like to miss anything and often plays receptionist. Behind O'Keeffe's throne-chair are copper-plated façades, hidden cupboards where he stores reams of materials and fabrics that make up the stuff of his trade.

Gabhan's creative need for self-expression traces back to his early lifeblood childhood passion: music. Entering his world of interiors was a natural creative progression. He can't recall his first exact interior scheme but reels off some famous names of actors to fill the void. O'Keeffe claims that every project is most memorable. 'Whatever the interior becomes, or whatever the personality and lifestyle evoke in me, is what my response is, and that's how it ends up.'

So what, I wonder, is the biggest compliment a client has ever awarded him?

'I receive letters all the time from happy people. But perhaps what was really lovely was being asked to share the initial pleasure of seeing the finished apartment with one particular client. She wanted me to be there to indulge the moment.'

I am reminded that O'Keeffe's clients never have to live with the builders but can afford to just turn the key when it's all over. Gabhan and his famous clients demonstrate a mutual disdain for anything that might compromise art and self-expression or create a diluted end result. 'What is this word budget? I keep meaning to look it up in the dictionary or somewhere to finally find out what it really means', he grins.

When I press Gabhan on why and how the life of an interior evolves to fit the personality and the lifestyle, how the brief is developed and the client researched, he shakes his head. 'It's instinct: I can tell after the first meeting whether or not it will work?' It is hard for Gabhan to explain how an interior evolves.

'Each imaged interior has a life of its own. It has a communication with the client and it's different from client to client.'

Famous people have famous egos to feed. Sometimes there appears no humanity in celebrity icons, almost by definition. They live through the media. They fulfil society's need for idols. So how is it for him, a creative artist, working with another creative artist or prima donna? Do atmospheres develop or life issues related to stardom - like sex, drugs and the rock and roll world in which he works - appear? Does he ever recognise that haunted look many icons wear as they deal with the pressures that fame brings?

'No', comes the straight answer. 'Of course, one is aware of the reality of extremities; that a client may be eating too little or too much, or drinking too little or too much, or sleeping too little or sleeping too much. That judgement arrives from one's own instinct and life patterns. How does one find the right partner and stay with them?' He answers his own question. 'One just does. The trick lies in recognising when something is right and staying with it.'

For Gabhan that is one of those funny questions he doesn't think about when he is working. When he's working, sharing the most intimate details of a client's life, he doesn't think ' She's drinking too much Southern Comfort'. This designer chooses not to have prejudices about his clients' lifestyles.

The spotlight has been on models, rock stars and fashion designers; now the focus is interior designers emerging themselves as celebrities.

Gabhan O'Keeffe is creating his own tempo, his own interior music at a heightened temperature for a limited and spell-bound audience. Perhaps his voice is small in a world that is bland and repetitive and headed in another direction. It seems that the individuality Gabhan values holds little value in today's global village. But in the niche market that has become his livelihood he can associate with the fantasy of life alongside other colourful and like-minded individuals. For Gabhan is brave enough to mould interiors that cocoon the feelings of these people and record all that is happening round about them. This is his time and he chooses not to take himself too seriously.

PORTRAIT INTERIORS

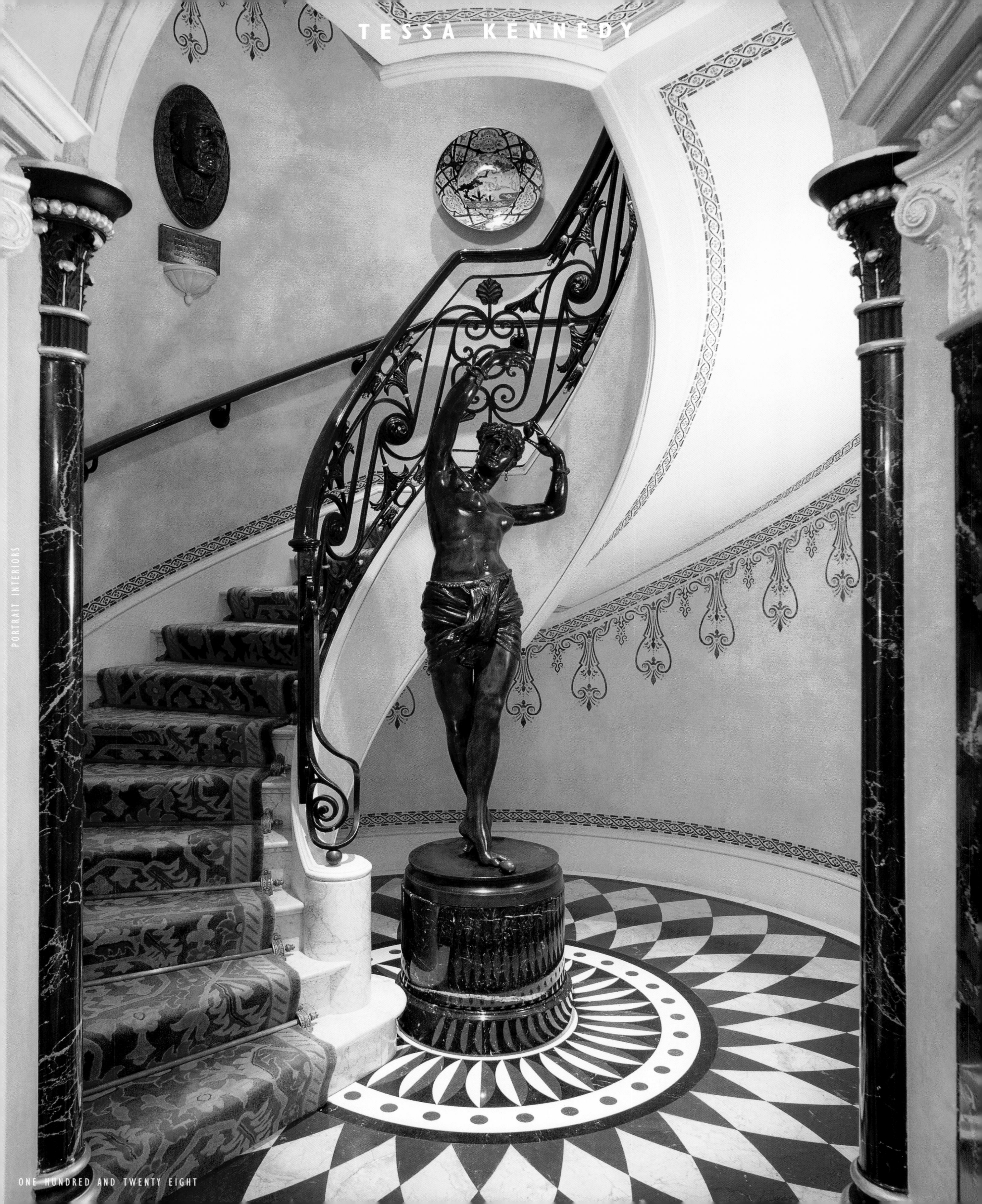

TESSA KENNEDY

Tessa Kennedy directs her interiors with passion and dedication. Her infinite imagination delivers glamorous special effects into her cultured world of interiors. Tessa Kennedy's celebrity clients much appreciate her innovative and thrilling designs; they trust in her artistic visions, and the environments she creates challenge each audience to rethink its own. This designer is only comfortable wearing a coat of many colours and its textured multiplicity has become her artistic statement. Tessa Kennedy's recent crafting behind the architectural façade of Aspinall's Club in the heart of Mayfair exposes some of her design mystery. Aspinall's is where Princes and Princesses of Darkness come to life; dramatic room sets reflect and service the passions of gambling pursuits. Each one staged to a central theme and acted out within a theatre of gilt, stained glass, heavy design detail and fantastic artefacts. Aspinall's aspires to the typically bold Tessa Kennedy difference and presents a rainbow pot of crafted luxury. The interior cocoons its members from bland reality and takes them on a round-the-world fantasy trip set in regal opulence.

What key associations spring to mind when you hear the word design?

Any mention of design makes me smile and think of beauty, luxury, scale, grandeur and detail.

Why has the Tessa Kennedy team grown to incorporate a professional team of architects, project managers and sub-contractors rather than keeping a focused eye on pure design?

By taking complete control of a project we deliver the best results for the client. We are not trained architects; perhaps that's why words like 'not possible' do not enter our professional vocabulary. The only boundaries are the realms of our imagination.

What is the most memorable project brief a client has delivered?

Each one is memorable in its own right. Our latest project at Aspinall's Club in Mayfair really stretched my imagination because we were presented with an empty shell and were not restricted by the client at all.

During childhood did you demonstrate the need for visual and kinaesthetic self-expression or enjoy any artistic pastimes that ultimately led you into the design field?

For as long as I can remember, I have been drawing, painting, designing and making things; collages, paintings, decorating doll's houses and designing their clothes.

Have modern advances in the fields of travel, technology and communication influenced your design approach?

I find as a result of all these things the world has shrunk. I am constantly searching the globe for new ideas and new inspirations.

Your design style has been described as 'eclectic' and 'opulent'. Are you comfortable with this reputation?

Definitely.

Does this career allow you to indulge your life passions?

Yes, I love to travel and shop and try to live life to the ultimate.

What magic spell does Russia cast over your personal theatre of design inspiration and taste?

Russia has had an enormous influence on my life. Rudolf Nureyev was my greatest friend for over 20 years. His first love was dancing, his second, less well-known passion, was shopping and his third was watching movies. My idea of heaven was to spend an evening in his company. I was always spellbound watching him dance and afterwards we would go for dinner before window shopping our way home to catch the late night films. We could often be found whiling away the hours watching Chinese Kung Fu movies in a Leicester Square film house - Rudolf was addicted to the action.

What is the best part of your daily job?

Making the client happy. It is always rewarding towards the end of a project, when everything starts coming together and the fruits of your labour blossom into a reality.

What sense do you rely upon when absorbed in design?

Instinct 100%.

Do guru design minds ever think alike?

No, but we like to stretch each other to the limits.

How does one stay 'creatively' fresh and inspired in design?

By always embracing something new. I never could attempt the same project twice because I would die of boredom.

Most of your work originates from repeat clients, yet the project range is diverse in nature. Do clients only love and respect you for your creative mind?

I hope not! They understand that I deliver a job on time and to budget but still manage to catch them out with the beauty of it all.

What emotions and messages should a successful interior convey to any host and invited guests?

Awesome.

Is it possible to explore the natural world for inspiration and, if so, where do you recommend?

From Savannah in Africa to the lochs and forests in Scotland, sunsets on the Nile, the ocean in Malibu, the lakes in Maine, the emerald coast of Turkey, the turquoise coast of Croatia, the whales in Newfoundland. Butterflies, birds, bugs, and marble quarries.

What is your penultimate design statement to date?

Avoid beige like the plague.....
Avoid white like the plague.....

PORTRAIT INTERIORS

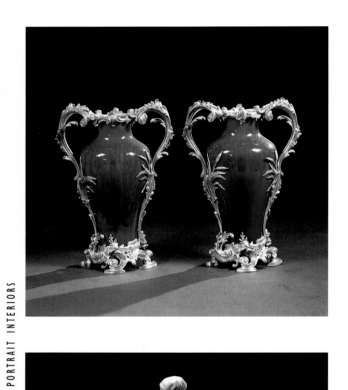

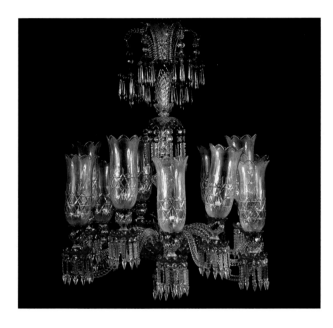

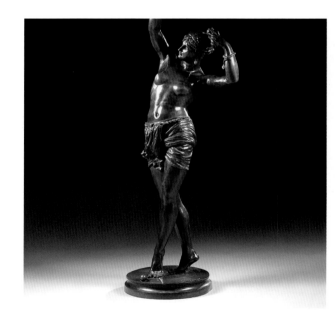

ASPINALL'S CLUB

PORTRAIT INTERIORS

When London's grandest jeweller in Bond Street needed an interior decorator, he summoned Andrè de Cacqueray. This designer's noble mark is gilded in gold and white and his crafting is symbolic of Europe's elite. Andrè de Cacqueray is an art historian by education, antique dealer by trade and interior decorator by inclination. His clients form part of a cultured jet set; they trek deeper into today's global village and return to be seduced by the charming instincts of this French classicist based in Chelsea. Andrè de Cacqueray spends his days managing an antique and design business and his nights recharging in his 19th-century chateau in the heart of SW1. Its space is a shrine dedicated to Louis XV period decoration and design detail. Andrè de Cacqueray has an almost magical ability to recreate the atmosphere and essence of French court and European heritage.

What brings a Frenchman to London?

London is a special place. Based here, I work with fabulous clients from all over the world. Somehow, when people come to London they develop a sense of freedom. They really want to live their lives and self-express through their interiors. Paris is a different city and different culture: it resembles a big stage set for the enjoyment of its inhabitants.

Do you miss the Parisian way?

I never really left Paris. An invisible umbilical cord pulls me back to my apartment there every few weeks. By living in England and travelling back to France for business, I have formed a better understanding of my own country. I am constantly developing my own sense of French culture: my instinctive style, my accent and my work.

Looking around your Kensington apartment makes the 'sheer interior nothing' of minimalism look so extreme. Is your French apartment decorated in the same way?

Yes. I once tried to live in a modern flat but it felt so unfriendly. Gradually, my antiques crept back in and eventually I gave all my modern things away. Minimalism is only perfect as minimalism: the moment you add something you ruin it.

You have a clear signature stamped all over your work but what makes your approach to decoration appealing?

My ideas add a bit of history and a bit of mystery. My clients love the fact that I know some old tricks, something different. In this world of interiors, it is not about finding the money to buy the design, it is about finding the right idea and the right designer to make it happen. My rooms don't need to be identical - I like to create different moods for different settings. For me, creating the mood is more important than the decoration.

Can you give a couple of examples?

I love to provide clients with a proper dressing room; designed in wood and arranged like a shop. Setting aside a separate room for the art of dressing provides a constant and daily pleasure. Dressing and undressing in a massive bedroom with tiny cupboards means constant tidying up because the act itself causes a mess. Creating 'his' and 'hers' bathrooms is another interesting idea. I am currently working on this with a client who has a small hotel of historic importance.

What do clients expect of you?

Anyone who comes to an interior designer is looking for a bit of fantasy; they're looking for someone to realise their dreams. I try to express people's dreams, I encourage clients to get a bit excited and help them to visualise ideas with me.

How do you work with colour?

Gold and white working together is symbolic of an elitist luxury from another time. People often confuse brass with gold. Correctly gilded gold cannot be compared with brass; gold attracts and retains light in a unique way. The function and circulation of an interior is more important than the colour. Generally, I like to work with three additional colours rather than two in a room. If a client wants red then I make a selection of reds; it is not difficult to match families of colour and the exact tone is not important. Ladies are much more exacting about colour. Sometimes, if that single factor becomes an obsession it can handicap a whole project.

How do you view what you do?

It is possible to live without an interior designer. So if a person selects an interior designer it is an extra luxury in their life: a hobby and a pleasure and often a very personal relationship between the two develops. I usually have an animated dialogue with clients because when someone asks you to make their home beautiful, they want it to work and they want you to do it well. Home is a place to make a personal statement.

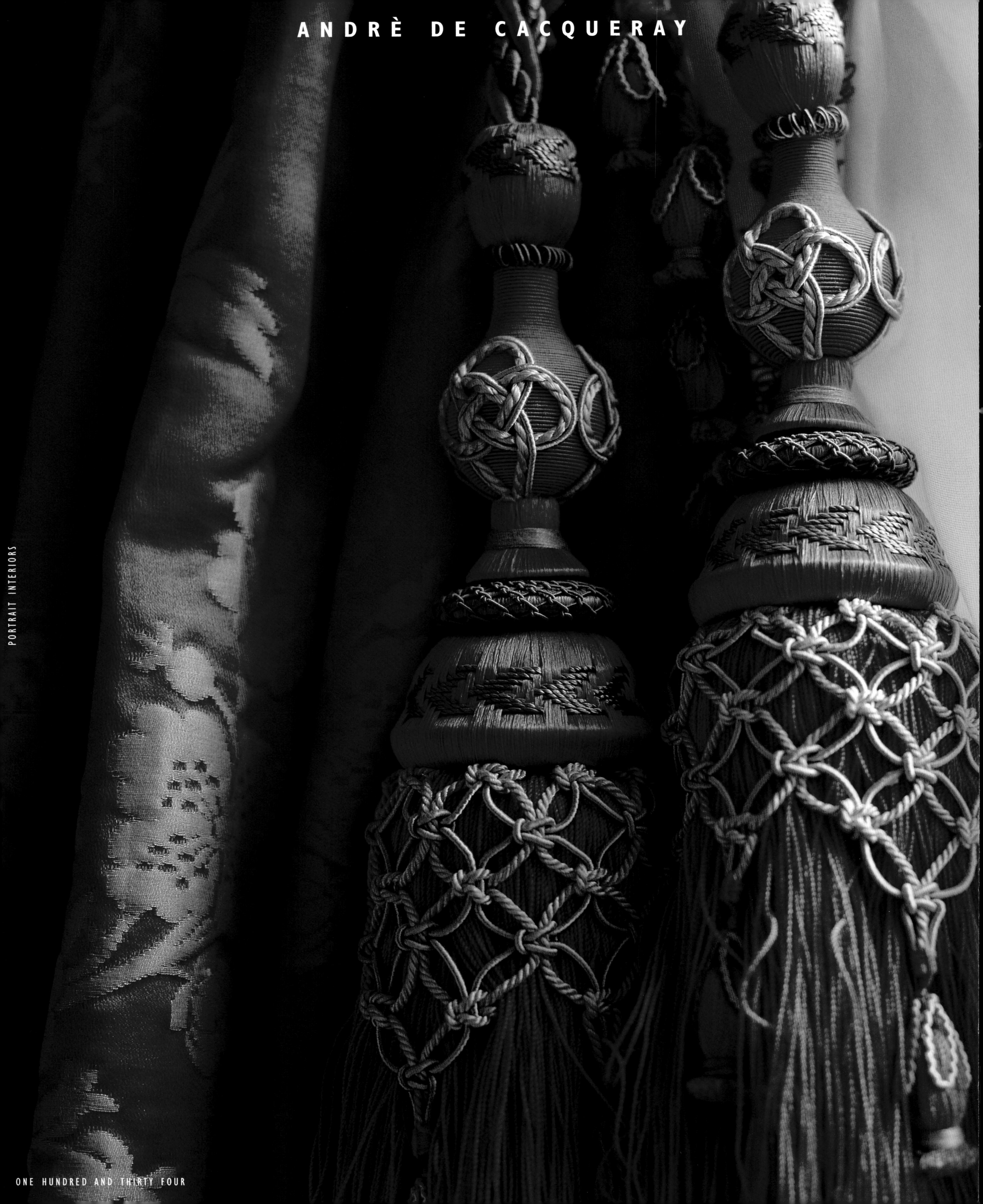

ANDRÈ DE CACQUERAY

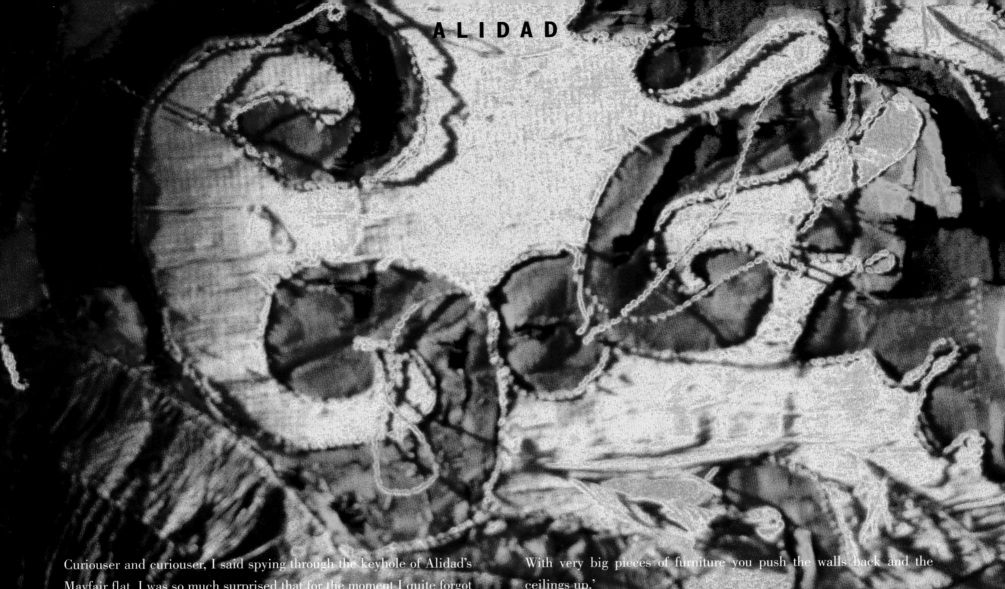

Curiouser and curiouser, I said spying through the keyhole of Alidad's Mayfair flat. I was so much surprised that for the moment I quite forgot to speak good English, unlike my Persian-born host, whose welcoming smile delivered me a perfectly manicured public-school greeting. Alidad, the gentleman, dismisses my faux-pas with an empathetic wave of the hand. Alidad, the designer, is used to creating love or hate first impressions; he understands that his style statement is a look to react to.

'Most people who approach me like my definite look and that makes life easier. I tell clients from the beginning that if they expect me to do something contemporary in one room and art nouveau in another I am not the right person. This is my style and it is elastic; it can be changed and modified to suit your requirement but within the look.'

It is an old look and one recently much admired; Alidad has frequently been awarded the coveted title of Best Interior Designer by leading glossy magazines. Such acclaim requires the artisan to open up his home as a showcase since Alidad's camera-shy clients never expose their treasured interiors for security reasons. As we turn the golden key to reveal his prized interior I feel like a falling Alice whose destination is Wonderland. For Alidad is passionate about over-scale and advises his companions to journey fearlessly down, down, down every decorating dream. In reality, Alidad operates like a meticulous cosmetic surgeon for the richest of the rich. Millionaires whose homes require lavish treatments like architectural face-lifts and decorative implants.

'If scale is not right, it can kill a room. If in doubt, over-scale: it always works. I usually go totally overboard! The first phase is to do the utmost architecturally. For example, I like to make very big openings to deceive the eye and make the room bigger. If a client has a very small room and wants it to look really special, I choose the biggest patterns I can find, the largest table or commode that will fit through the door.

With very big pieces of furniture you push the walls back and the ceilings up.'

Alidad's home exposes his life's travels and Persian roots, a culture that knows how to keep warm with layers of cloth and ancient heritage. It boasts trompe l'oeil walls and ceilings appear to recede into the distance; the antique furniture is on a grand scale; and there are faded antique textiles in abundance. The result is a potent interior that merits slow digestion. 'Perhaps Alidad's show-flat has heritage listing' I think to myself in a dreamy sort of way, sinking deep between endless velvet cushions and drinking in the heady effects of this inviting sitting room. It is easy to envelop yourself in the cosy mix of textures. Soft velvets in shades of tomato red heat up the battered cream leathers, well-worn Persian carpet, plain linen sofa and faded 17th-century wall hanging. A typical Alidad interior presents itself as a candle-lit illusion that in truth is illuminated by state of the art 21st-century fibre optics. The atmosphere generated is electric, yet I feel soothed by mellow candle-light and a glowing fire; such ambience creates inner warmth and banishes the cold realities of the outside world.

No matter how comfortable the special effects, flow and function are always Alidad's top creative priority. The designer's starting point is a floor plan to see how to make the space work. He ensures that each public room he crafts can cater for the maddest mad hatter tea-party.

'People are often so busy thinking about how to make the room look beautiful that function is the last thing on their minds. It's important to visualise someone coming into the room with a tea tray - where will they put it? How will they pour the tea? Where will the guests put their cups down?'

Alidad approaches his professional role like a counsellor.

'I listen to how a room talks. Every room has a story and I listen to its story. In the beginning I spend a lot of time with clients. I encourage

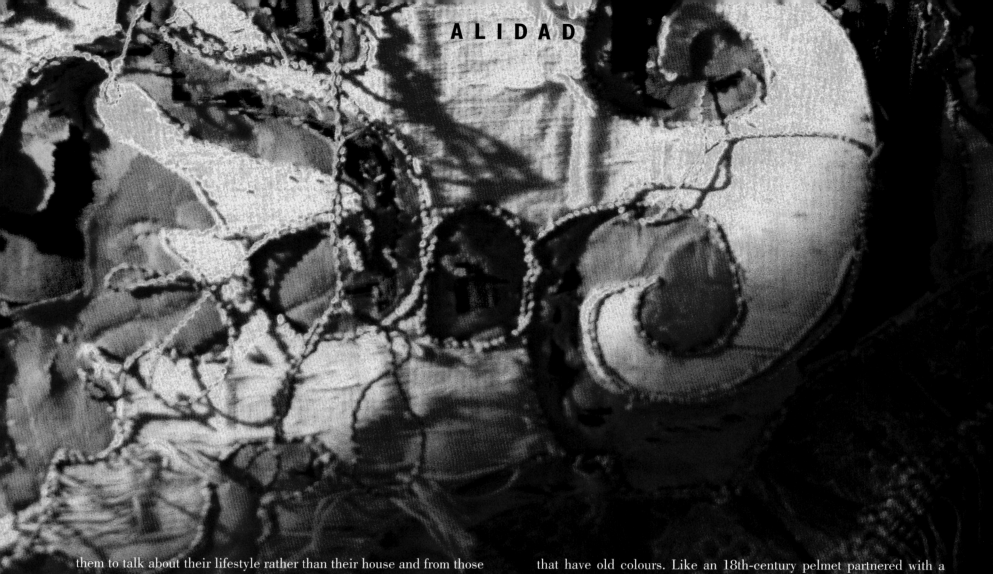

them to talk about their lifestyle rather than their house and from those conversations I find key words to store away. I slowly begin to understand that they hate that sort of thing or they really love that sort of thing.'

Somewhere along the communication path, Alidad instinctively develops a full sense of the aura he should conjure up within the interior space. The beginning is often complicated, particularly because the majority of his projects require the designing of bespoke tailored wall-covering and fabrics.

'When everything is made from scratch, I find old documents in fabric factories that haven't been used for a while. I find that by changing the colour things come out very differently. Today's fabric shops take an old design and reduce the scale of the pattern in keeping with a trend away from large designs. I go right back to the original and keep the scale so that it remains sympathetic to the way it was.'

That difference has huge decorative impact on the overall scheme.

'I like the textures to be layered as if everything has been built up over the years. It is an evolved look that is not just a combination of great inherited art but also involves something plastic.'

For Alidad synthetics help to encapsulate an interior's soul and express life's journey. He enjoys mixing the gravitas of treasured antiques with the gayness of life's baubles.

'I am not a purist in that respect. When people are very rigid it bores me to death. I am not trying to create a museum: I have to have my plastics.'

To take all the fabrics from an Alidad room and put them all together on a sample board would be a 'horrific' experience. Yet en masse and in situ they work well. And it is Alidad's play on patterns that ultimately creates his opulent look.

'I do have a lot of patterns, there's no doubt about it. Sometimes every single fabric is old. What I currently enjoy is mixing in modern fabrics

that have old colours. Like an 18th-century pelmet partnered with a brand new modern textured weave.'

Most designers true colours shine through their craft. Alidad designs imply that for him red is always the centre and lifeblood of his interiors. Understanding Alidad's use of colour is like slotting into place the central piece of a complex puzzle.

'If anything I am colour blind,' he confesses. 'If I am using red, I mix up plenty of different reds and think only of the overall image of the room. It becomes like a canvas. I start off adding colour and keep on standing back. I might need a little more green here and a little deep red there.'

The decorative goal is simple. Alidad wants people to remain comfortably within the interior walls of his illusion.

'I can't bear places where the cushions are so puffed up that you are afraid to sit down,' he politely yawns. Alidad appears suddenly tired by the telling of his own tale. 'It is so difficult to convey the atmosphere of my rooms because they work on the principle of all five senses.'

In truth, he is right. Experiencing the Alidad design impact is a subliminal affair and the camera lens dilutes its synergy. The designer's interior flirting works best in a womb-like setting of soft velvets, crunchy chenilles and warm wools, choral music, scent-infused candles and tempting nibbles. Alidad's statement is a sixth sense fable about atmosphere and instinct that ends with the assurance that his creative best is yet to come.

As we part at the door of his Mayfair stately home, I step back into the harsh reality of a London street. And Alidad? Alidad patiently awaits another adventurous Alice, eager and bored by the realities of her mundane life. And, when tomorrow's Alice does appear, I hope she arrives flush from a win on the lottery. That way she'll come equipped to do justice to Alidad's decorative dream.

ALIDAD

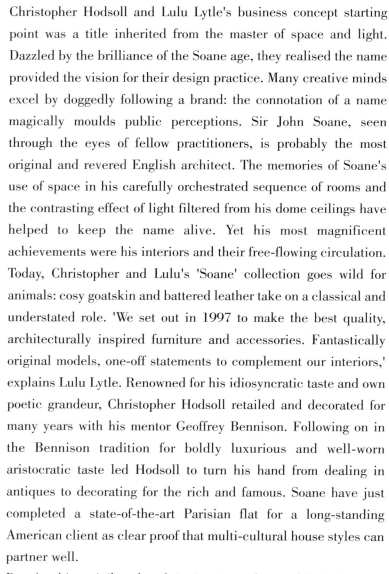

Christopher Hodsoll and Lulu Lytle's business concept starting point was a title inherited from the master of space and light. Dazzled by the brilliance of the Soane age, they realised the name provided the vision for their design practice. Many creative minds excel by doggedly following a brand: the connotation of a name magically moulds public perceptions. Sir John Soane, seen through the eyes of fellow practitioners, is probably the most original and revered English architect. The memories of Soane's use of space in his carefully orchestrated sequence of rooms and the contrasting effect of light filtered from his dome ceilings have helped to keep the name alive. Yet his most magnificent achievements were his interiors and their free-flowing circulation. Today, Christopher and Lulu's 'Soane' collection goes wild for animals: cosy goatskin and battered leather take on a classical and understated role. 'We set out in 1997 to make the best quality, architecturally inspired furniture and accessories. Fantastically original models, one-off statements to complement our interiors,' explains Lulu Lytle. Renowned for his idiosyncratic taste and own poetic grandeur, Christopher Hodsoll retailed and decorated for many years with his mentor Geoffrey Bennison. Following on in the Bennison tradition for boldly luxurious and well-worn aristocratic taste led Hodsoll to turn his hand from dealing in antiques to decorating for the rich and famous. Soane have just completed a state-of-the-art Parisian flat for a long-standing American client as clear proof that multi-cultural house styles can partner well.

Despite his privileged upbringing into the world of interiors Hodsoll doesn't bang on about antique integrity or pompous creativity.

'People like to mix our new stuff with our old stuff; our modern Soane designs with our Bennison antiques', he says. Hodsoll's Pimlico retail window displays demonstrate a highly individual and inventive use of space.

'The look is always high impact', explains Lulu.

'Christopher really attacks space quickly and has an immediate vision of what he wants to achieve. He is brilliant at creating that Soane feeling of incredible scale in a room. His spaces project a sense of grandness without being at all intimidating'.

Soane commissions British artisans to craft classically inspired architectural furniture and accessories. Partner Lulu Lytle scoured the country to track down masters of technique who could help them bring a client's interior to life with passion and style.

'Our most extraordinary contact is the Dorset quarry man who never holds any one hundred and thirty million years old 'forming fossils' in stock. Permanently covered in a film of white dust, he bespoke quarries for each Jurassic lamp we order. International clients recognise the quality of Soane master-crafted designs to be the best in the world.'

PORTFOLIO GALLERY

ANTHONY FELDMAN

Mayfair is to architecture what Bond Street is to retail: within yards of each other live some of the most famous designers in the business. They are seduced by its history and prestige. Architect Anthony Feldman lives in the building site he's renovating in the heart of Mayfair; he can't imagine a more ideal home environment. Looking down from his roof terrace and listening to Feldman is a revelation: a great way to survey the changing profile of buildings below. Mayfair designers are a special breed. They are as comfortable on a loft apartment couch as they are in royal palaces. They are as familiar with the interiors of private jets as they are used to journeying way beyond at a moment's notice. Some, like Nicky Haslam, dress up for the design icon part. Others are low-key. Anthony Feldman may be the demure architect who travels light years away from a glitzy approach but he is Mayfair's local hero. When he took me walkabouts, to further introduce me to his ways of seeing, everyone knew charismatic Anthony and Feldman chatted wherever we went. 'I think that conversation is very important. As an architect you become the impetus behind things. If the solution is going to be brilliant or interesting it is because you have dragged everybody together and brought that recipe into being.' Feldman studied his architecture in Bedford Square and is genuinely passionate about the subject. He is constantly striving to recreate the environment, shaping the space in which we live, imposing a little order and beauty upon a world often more familiar with ugliness and disorder. 'There is nothing nicer than completing a project on time and to budget. It's like producing the Sunday roast to perfection, all crunchy and juicy. I love the sense of pleasure when you pull off the timing.' Feldman is a trained classical pianist and 'undercover' chef. For him learning to cook is like designing interiors. 'You learn that some ingredients like tomatoes, onions and garlic just go naturally together.'

Feldman endures a constant passion to correct things that feel wrong; he cannot remember a time when he was not interested in stuff and its arrangement. 'If I stay in a hotel and the furniture layout isn't right I have to swoop it around; sometimes whole corridors get involved.' Feldman understands there can be a price to pay for adapting interiors according to his inclination. 'We were staying in India at the Lake Palace Hotel,' he recalls. 'To my horror, our room's furniture was lined up along one side, like a doctor's waiting room. Within minutes, I had rearranged everything and a hundred candles were lit. We flung the windows open to breathe in paradise. Five minutes later 10 million mosquitoes from the lake, attracted by the light, took up our 'dinner' invitation. It took the maintenance people days to mop up the invading bodies.'

ANTHONY FELDMAN

1. 18 Hertford Street built by Henry Holland in the 1780s.
2. Chesterfield Hill via Curzon Street cinema passing Beau Brummel's house.
3. Up to Farm Street and into the Farm Street Church (altar screen by Giles Gilbert Scott).
4. Into St George's Gardens: an outdoor series of rooms.
5. Past the Grosvenor Chapel (1730) and into Thomas Goode: view the stained glass, bird murals and small museum of porcelain dinner plates produced over the last century.
6. Past Purdey to Richoux.

Anthony Feldman's Mayfair Guide

PORTFOLIO GALLERY

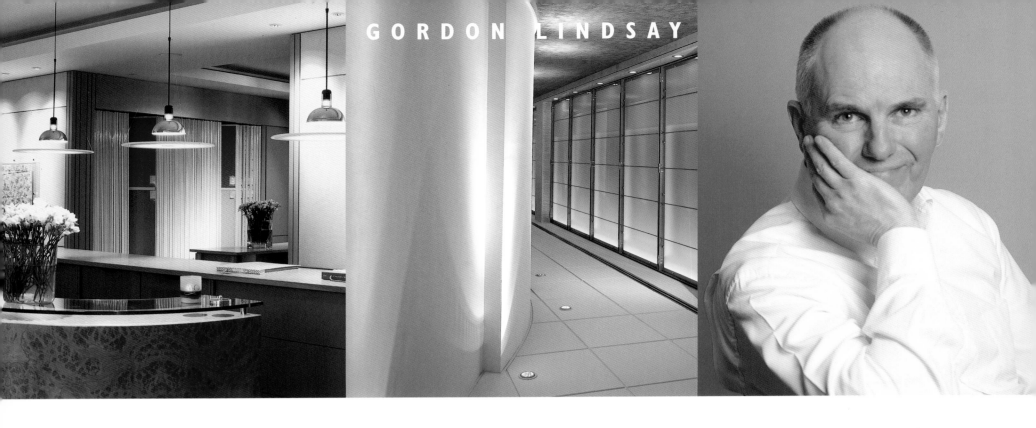

Stage-struck Gordon Lindsay came to London for the drama of window dressing and found interior design waiting in the wings. Lindsay started out studying textiles at Manchester Art School because 'there was no such thing as an interior design course in the fifties' and has worked to raise interiors from a schmaltzy interlude to dramatic device. He introduced his passionate knowledge of theatrical sets to the face of seventies retail, claiming that 'the closed windows and stage sets of the high street' originally attracted him to the art. 'Window dressing then was very disciplined; everything was pressed and immaculate.' Lindsay became 'the northern Rottweiler' and was sent out to bring problem C&A branches to heel. 'The 25 resident gum-chewing staff at Marble Arch greeted me with laughter - they joked that I'd come straight off the set at Coronation Street. It was only after I fired five of them that we got a really good team going.' By the end of the seventies, Lindsay realised that such initial callings had been misplaced and his compulsion to make sets and create stories finally translated into new jargon 'interior design.' His Gordon Lindsay Partnership became the flagship design and decoration business in West London. Lindsay's reputation today is as a die-hard campaigner for his profession: he wants to professionally tag design and standardise the realm of decoration with key 'building' rules.

Gordon Lindsay believes you can improve the world of interiors. Design matters. Just don't forget the three C's - coats, coffee and chips. Work quickly, keep the creative mind unlocked, work whenever. Know when to work alone and when to work together. Share ideas, thoughts and dreams. Trust your colleagues. No politics and no bureaucracy. Sign a contract. The client defines a job well done. Radical ideas are not bad ideas. Invent different ways of seeing. Make a contribution every day. If it doesn't contribute to the profession leave it behind.

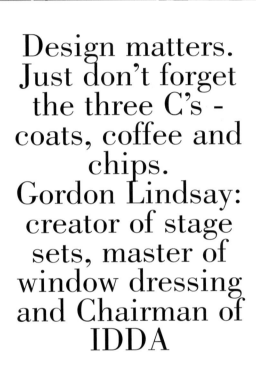

Design matters.
Just don't forget
the three C's -
coats, coffee and
chips.
Gordon Lindsay:
creator of stage
sets, master of
window dressing
and Chairman of
IDDA

Lavinia Dargie's decorating style retains strong echoes of a childhood spent in India and the Far East. The fusion of cultures translates into her vibrant and individual marque. 'A love of rich colours and diversity of textures was indelibly imprinted on me and I have always used them, albeit sparingly, so that they never overpower a Western setting.' That look fits well into today's contemporary world of interiors; a reflective market passionately concerned with East-West furnishings and objets d'art. Her early professional life was spent in the international fast lane of Hong Kong's advertising sector and provided her with focused business training. 'In advertising, you present the visuals, understand budgets, become persuasive and learn to be disciplined in your approach - it was a great foundation.'

Today, Lavinia Dargie's pitch is interiors; clients and fellow professionals respect the designer as a team player and value her up-front approach. 'The secret when you work with architects is to immediately ask them about their ground rules - how do they want to work? Some are interested in design and others are not. I always establish at the very beginning what is expected from me.'

Lavinia's London-based studio, Dargie Lewis, was founded during the mid-seventies. Culturally, the design ethos combines strong, uncluttered lines with attention to detail and a generous use of well-toned fabrics. The designer constantly draws on an innate ability to recall colour, spatial dimensions and interior proportions. Global travel also plays an influential role in her creative development.

'Each time I go away something inspires me,' says Lavinia. Her most recent stay was in a Montana log cabin, set amongst a multitude of wild flowers and alien terrain. Not a typically conventional residential interior, but the warmth, colours, atmosphere and layout prompted her to stop, look, listen and learn.

Back in London, Lavinia's design studio functions best as a small team. The structure allows her to deal with everyone on a personal basis. 'Clients must feel that they have created their own, individual look. You have to know how they live, work, play and entertain. The design must complement their lifestyle and favourite artefacts rather than imposing on them. This avoids the contrived designer look and allows me freedom to add spontaneous touches that put the real soul into every setting.'

LAVINIA DARGIE

'The art of decorating is knowing when to stop. Simplicity is always best,' says designer Lavinia Dargie. 'The cardinal virtue of all beauty is restraint.'

ELSIE DE WOLFE

'EVERYBODY IS SO FRANTIC TODAY: *I believe that we all want to come*
home to a sanctuary, a place to re-charge not face great challenge'.
Lynne Hunt

Sheer blonde interiors press the button without raising the alarm. Lynne Hunt designs dark blonde spaces that invoke natural glamour rather than provoke brassy intimidation. They symbolise youth and warm summer rays, they boost energy and restore harmony, they function like a soothing balm anointed to over-stretched senses. 'Everybody is so frantic nowadays and I believe that we all want to come home to a sanctuary, a place to recharge not face great challenge'.

Hunt travelled extensively during childhood and absorbed cross-culturing first hand. She demonstrates an easy cosmopolitan philosophy and is respected for crafting some world-class havens. Her signature spells out the scent of student design days spent in hazy Californian sunshine on Long Beach; a setting of long hair, long legs, long smiles, long drinks, long horizons and long blonde looks. But for all that exposure to exoticism and sumptuousness, Hunt's designs ultimately respect each project's own environment and lifestyle agenda. Her edge is contemporary, with modern sun-kissed finishes that sparkle like spun gold. The colour palette shimmers like textured sand; caramel on honey, oatmeal on wheat germ, lemon on vanilla, camomile on sunflower, platinum on champagne. Hunt uses grainy materials to sculpt designs into an asymmetrical free-form shape, to attract interest and arouse basic instincts. Her versatile solutions are gently delivered with a style that is unafraid to cut loose and ooze funky, chunky appeal.

PORTFOLIO GALLERY

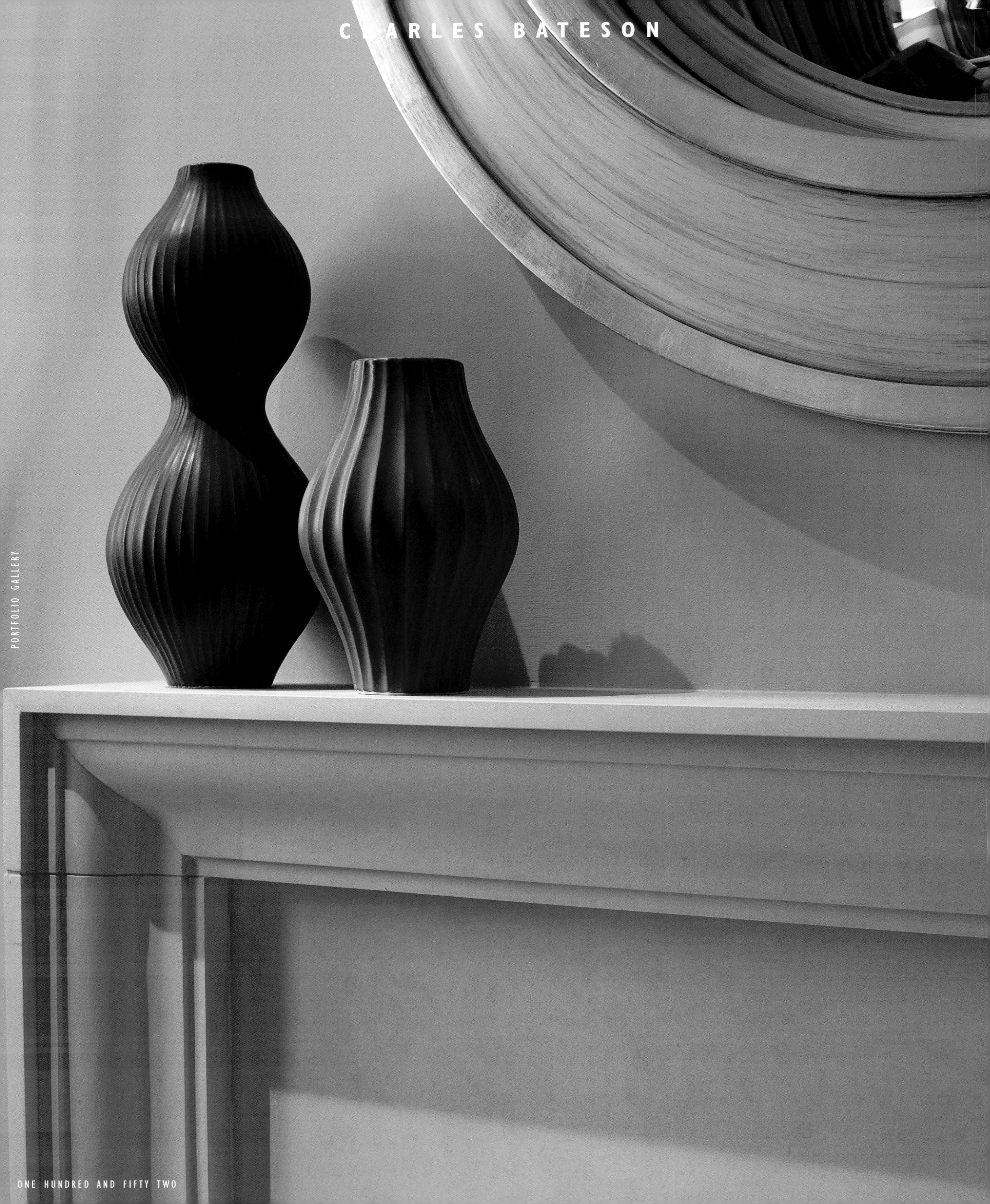

Elegant lines, dynamic statements and exceptional style set the marque of Charles Bateson and his design mentors. The lures, the achievements, the eccentricities of designers, decorators and architects mould the shape of our built environment. Half a century ago, the simple philosophy of David Hicks engraved a vibrant tattoo on the shoulder of 18th-century grandeur. Hicks' injection of new character remains the quintessence of smart taste. Since homes can become prisons we need to learn freedom in the way we decorate them. Contemporary designer Bateson pulls out the crown jewels borrowed from his old master to give them a thorough dusting. His work pays homage to Hicks' signature and the maestro himself. His interior strategy is to try to understand the essence of why rather than what. One can grow accustomed to ugliness, but never to carelessness. Bateson's fitting lines bring new energy and reflection - this is the same home but crafted for a third millennium setting.

PORTFOLIO GALLERY

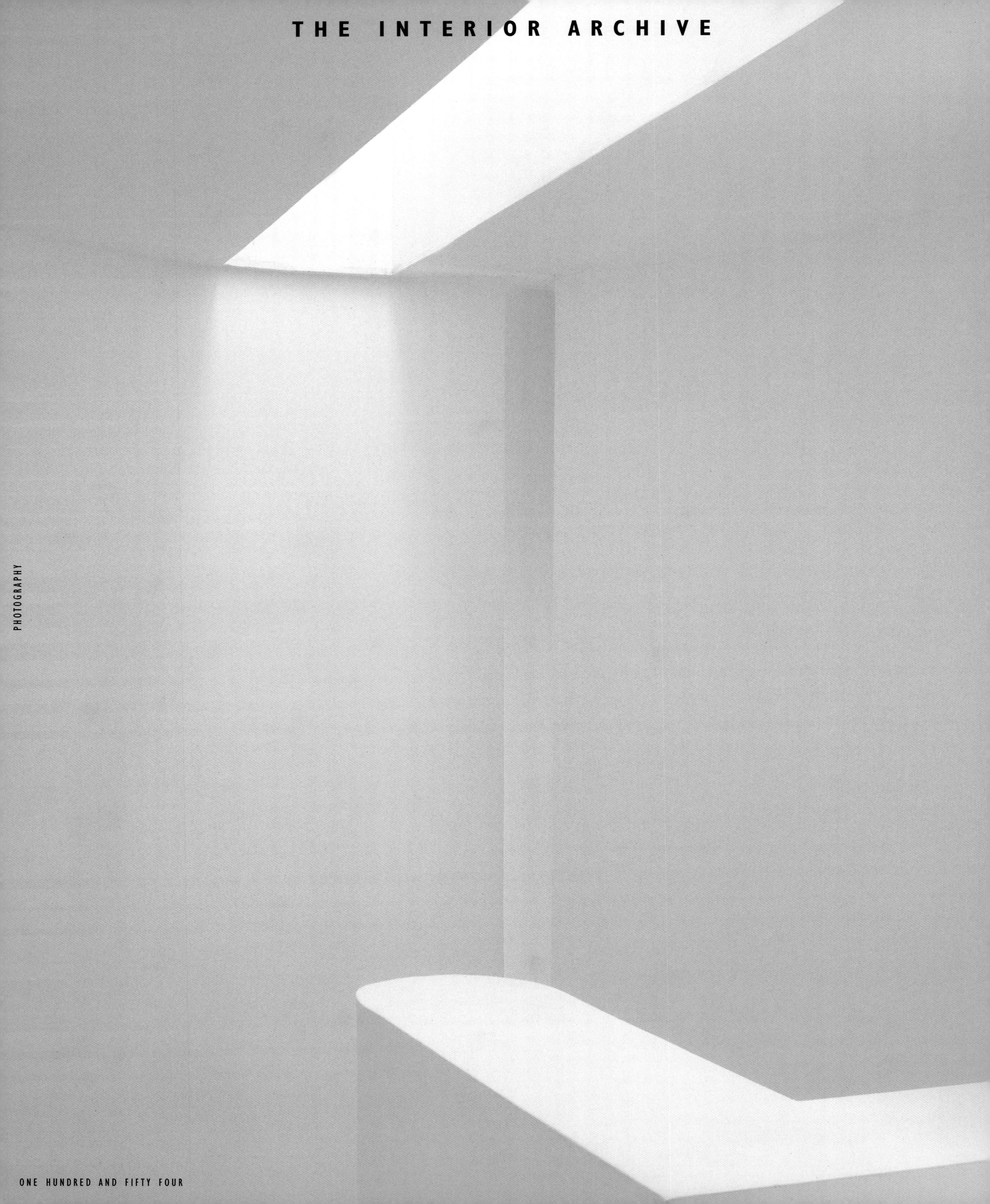

PHOTOGRAPHY

FRONT COVER:
Photography by Simon Upton @ Interior Archive
Courtesy of Dolce & Gabbana
Property: Domenico Dolce and Stefano Gabbana's
Milanese Villa, Italy
FRONT COVER FLAP
Words by Carolynne Murphy
BACK COVER:
Designers in profile
BACK COVER FLAP:
Portrait by Paul Chave
Words by Carolynne Murphy

PREFACE

PAGES 6-7
Words by Carolynne Murphy

FOREWORD

PAGES 8-9
Words by The Right Honourable Lord
Sheppard of Didgemere, KCVO
Chairman of London First
London First
1 Hobhouse Court
Suffolk Street
London SW1Y 4HH
T: 020 7665 1500
F: 020 7665 1501
www.london-first.co.uk
www.lfc.co.uk

PHOTOGRAPHY

PAGES 10-11
Photography by Fritz von der
Schulenburg @ The Interior Archive
Architect: Charles Rennie Mackintosh
The Interior Archive Limited
15 Grand Union Centre, West Row
London W10 5AS
T: 020 7370 0595
F: 020 8960 2695
www.interiorarchive.com

DESIGN REDISCOVERY

PAGES 12-13
Photography by Fritz von der
Schulenburg and James Mortimer @
The Interior Archive
Property: The Arab Hall, Leighton
House

PAGE 15
Opening inspired by David Mlinaric
Mlinaric, Henry and Zervudachi Limited
38 Bourne Street
London SW1W 8JA
T: 020 7730 9072
F: 020 7823 4756

PAGE 16
Portrait by Fritz von der Schulenburg
@ The Interior Archive
PAGE 17
An introduction to David Mlinaric

PAGES 18-19
Photography by Fritz von der
Schulenburg @ The Interior Archive
Property: Studio apartment, Chelsea,
London

PAGES 20-21
An interview with David Mlinaric

PAGES 22-23
Photography by Mark Fiennes
Property: Spencer House
Kind permission from Her Majesty The
Queen, The Tate Gallery, London 2000, The
Victoria & Victoria & Museum's Loans
Spencer House
27 St James's Place
London SW1A 1NR
T: 020 7514 1964
F: 020 7409 2952
www.spencerhouse.co.uk

PAGES 24-25
Photography by Andreas von Einsiedel
and Derry Moore @ The National
Trust Photographic Library
Property: Beningbrough Hall, North
Yorkshire, UK

DIRECTORY

PAGES 26
Portrait courtesy of Silver Cross Archive
PAGE 27
An interview with Jane Churchill
Jane Churchill Interiors Limited
81 Pimlico Road
London SW1W 8PH
T: 020 7730 8564
F: 020 7823 6421

PAGES 28-29
Photography courtesy of Silver Cross Archive
Silver Cross (1999) Limited
Otley Road
Guisley
Leeds LS20 8LP

PAGE 30
Portrait by Alaisdair Smith
PAGE 31
An Interview with Amanda Rosa
Amanda Rosa Interiors
26 Holland Street
Glasgow G2 4LR
Scotland, UK
T: 0141 227 6262
F: 0141 227 6263

PAGES 32-33
Photography by Alaisdair Smith
Property: Gleneagles Hotel
The Gleneagles Hotel
Auchterarder
Perthshire PH3 1NF
Scotland
UK
T: 01764 662231
F: 01764 662134
www.gleneagles.com

SEEDS OF CHANGE

PAGE 35
Wisdom of Alfred Lord Tennyson

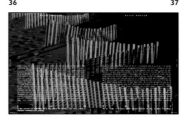

PAGES 36-37
Photography by Bill Batten.
Courtesy of Conran Octopus Limited
Kelly Hoppen Interiors
2 Munden Street
London W14 0RH
T: 020 7471 3350
F: 020 7471 3351

PAGE 38
Portrait by Bill Batten
Courtesy of Conran Octopus Limited
PAGE 39
Photography by Bill Batten.
Courtesy of Conran Octopus Limited

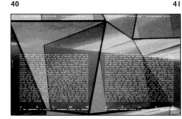

PAGE 40-41
Photography courtesy of Procter Rihl Archive
Procter Rihl
63 Cross Street
London N1 2BB
T: 020 7704 6003
F: 020 7688 0478
www.procter-rihl.com
info@procter-rihl.com

PAGE 42
Portrait from Procter Rihl Archive
PAGE 43
Photography by Sue Barr and Procter Rihl
Garden: Gardens sans Frontières at Chelsea Flower Show 2000
Designer: Ryl Nowell

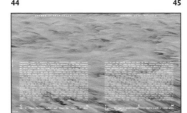

PAGES 44-45
Photography by Lee Frost @ The National Trust Photographic Library
Agenda 21 Architects
116-120 Golden Lane
Clerkenwell
London EC1Y 0TL
T: 020 7687 6001
F: 020 7687 6002
art@a21a.demon.co.uk

PAGES 46-47
Photography from Agenda 21 Architects Archive
Green lyrics inspired by Agenda 21 Architects

PAGE 48
Portrait from NH Design Archive
PAGE 49
Photography by Andrew Wood
Property: New Orleans House, USA
NH Design Architectural and Interior
91 Lower Sloane Street
London SW1W 8DA
T: 020 7730 0808
F: 020 7730 0888
n.h.design@btinternet.com

FANTASY

PAGES 50-51
Photography by Andrew Wood
Property: New Orleans House, USA
Fashion lyrics inspired by Nicky Haslam

PAGES 52-53
Photography by Stephen White courtesy of NMEC Archive
Property: The Body Zone at the Millennium Dome, London
John Hackney
38 Richmond Hill, Richmond TW10 6QX
T: 020 8940 2077
Dave Waters
41 Great Pulteney Street, London W1N 3DE
T: 020 7734 5888

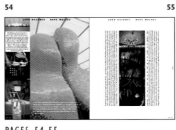

PAGES 54-55
Photography by Stephen White courtesy of NMEC and QA Archive
Property: The Body Zone at the Millennium Dome, London
Architects: Branson Coates
Interior design led by John Hackney and Dave Waters

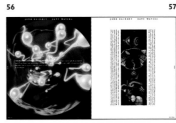

PAGE 56
Sperm Installation and Eye film courtesy of The Frame Store Archive, London
PAGE 57
Photography by Stephen White courtesy of NMEC Archive
Property: The Body Zone at the Millennium Dome, London

CREDITS AND CONTACTS

DIRECTORY

58  **59**

PAGES 58-59
Photography by Guy Marineau courtesy of Limelight and Christian Lacroix Archive
David Collins Architecture and Design
6-7 Chelsea Wharf Lots Road
London SW10 0QJ
T: 020 7349 5900
F: 020 7352 7284
studio@davidcollins.com

60  **61**

PAGES 60-61
Photography by Peter Aprahamian
Property: Madonna's Bedroom, House & Garden Fair 2000

62  **63**

PAGE 62
Portrait by Rick Guest
PAGE 63
Photography by Andrew Lambe
Property: La Tante Claire, London
Words by David Collins

64  **65**

PAGES 64-65
Photography by Tricia Guild extracted from 'White Hot' by Tricia Guild with Elspeth Thompson
Permission from Quadrille Publishing
Designers Guild
3 Olaf Street
London W11 4BE
T: 020 7243 7300
F: 020 7243 7320
www.designersguild.com

66  **67**

PAGES 66-67
Photography by James Merrell extracted from 'Cut Flowers' by Tricia Guild and 'White Hot' by Tricia Guild with Elspeth Thompson
Permission from Quadrille Publishing

68  **69**

PAGE 68
Portrait by James Merrell

PAGE 69
Words by Tricia Guild

70  **71**

PAGES 70-71
Photography by Jan Baldwin
Nina Campbell
7 Milner Street
London SW3 2QA
T: 020 7589 8589
F: 020 7589 2369

72  **73**

PAGES 72-73
Photography by Jan Baldwin, Christopher Simon Sykes and James Mortimer
Permission from House & Garden and The Condé Nast Publications Limited

74 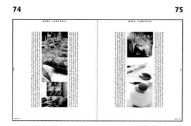 **75**

PAGES 74-75
Photography by Jan Baldwin, Christopher Simon Sykes and James Mortimer
Permission from House & Garden and The Condé Nast Publications Limited

76  **77**

PAGES 76-77
Photography by Andrew Lawson
Design of Hellabores 'song sheet' by Fiona Forsyth
Arabella Lennox-Boyd Landscape and Architectural Design
45 Moreton Street
London SW1V 2NY
T: 020 7931 9995
F: 020 7821 6585
www.arabellalennoxboyd.com
office@alboffice.edi.co.uk

78  **79**

PAGES 78-79
Photography by Arabella Lennox-Boyd, Andrew Lawson and Jerry Harpur
Gardens: Gresgarth Hall in Lancashire, private Chateau in France, Chelsea Flower Show 2000

80  **81**

PAGES 80-81
Photography by Andrew Lawson

WAYS OF SEEING

82  **83**

PAGES 82-83
Joanna Wood's inspirations
Nature: *Photography by Geoff du Feu @ The Telegraph Colour Library Archive*
Fabric: *Photography of chair detail courtesy of Mallett of London Archive*
Soane: *Photography courtesy of Sir John Soane's Museum Archive*

84  **85**

PAGE 84
An interview with Joanna Wood
PAGE 85
Photography from Joanna Wood's Archive
Joanna Trading
7 Bunhouse Place
London SW1W 8HU
T: 020 7730 0693
F: 020 7730 4135

86  **87**

PAGE 87
Photography by Fritz von der Schulenburg @ The Interior Archive
Property: Peterhof Throne Room

88 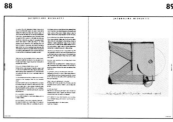 **89**

PAGE 88
An interview with Jacqueline Nicolotti
PAGE 89
Artwork with Islamic text 'A man's home is his universe'
Courtesy of Jacqueline Nicolotti's Archive
FSI plc
117 Old Brompton Road
London SW7 3RN
T: 020 7244 8671
F: 020 7370 3251
fsi@fsi.sonnet.co.uk

DIRECTORY

PAGE 90
An interview with Anthony Collett and Andrzej Zarzycki
PAGE 91
Photography by Richard Waite
Property: Old Church Street, London
Collett Zarzycki
Fernhead Studios
2B Fernhead Road
London W9 3ET
T: 020 8969 6967
F: 020 8960 6480
mail@czltd.co.uk

PAGES 92-93
Photography by Richard Waite and James Mortimer
London Properties: Old Church Street, Bath & Racquets Club, Christie's, Alembic House, Whistles, St James's Place and Paulton's Square.

PAGE 94
An interview with Philip Hooper
PAGE 95
Photography of the fossil by Fritz von der Schulenburg @ The Interior Archive
Philip Hooper Design Associates Limited & Jones Lambell Architecture and Design
Studio 30 The Old Latchmere School
38 Burns Road
London SW11 5GY
T: 020 7978 6662
F: 020 7223 3713

PAGES 96-97
Photography by Fritz von der Schulenburg @ The Interior Archive
Architects: Peter Jones and Ed Bowness @ Jones Lambell Architecture and Design
Property: Portobello Road, London
Words by Philip Hooper

PAGE 98
An interview with John Solomon and Colin Duckworth
PAGE 99
Photography by Henry Wilson
Property: London Apartment
John Solomon and Associates
Studio 13, The Coda Centre
Munster Road, London SW6 6AW
T: 020 7381 2766
F: 020 7386 0377
mail@jsajsd.com
www.jsajsd.com

DESIGN INNOVATION

PAGE 100
Portrait by Peter Anderson
PAGE 101
Photography by June Buck and Andreas von Einsiedel
Script by Justin Meath Baker
Meath Baker Design Partnersip
7 Barlow Place off Bruton Lane
London W1X 7AE
T: 020 7491 9900
F: 020 7491 9919
info@meathbakerdesign.demon.co.uk
www.meathbakerdesign.com

PAGE 102
Portrait from Mark Humphrey's Archive
PAGE 103
Drawing from Mark Humphrey's portfolio
Mark Humphrey Limited
L23 The Old Laboratory Studios
2 Michael Road
London SW6 2AD
T: 020 7348 7500
F: 020 7731 5858
enquiries@markhumphrey.co.uk
www.markhumphrey.co.uk

PAGE 104
Portrait by Jennifer Collins
PAGE 105
Photography by Jennifer Collins
MDID
103 Dundas Street
Edinburgh EH3 6SD
Scotland
T: 0131 558 1997
F: 0131 556 1998
design@mdid.co.uk
www.mdid.co.uk

PAGE 106-107
Photography by Jennifer Collins

PAGE 108
Portrait by Peter Bennett
PAGE 109
Photography by Peter Bennett
Nelson Design
169 St John's Hill
London SW11 1TQ
T: 020 7924 4542
F: 020 7924 5342
info@nelsondesign.co.uk

PAGES 110-111
Photography by Graham Challifour

PAGES 112-113
Photography by Peter Bennett
Property: Carlton Garden, London
Developer: Benchmark Group plc

PAGE 114
Portrait by Tim Hall
PAGE 115
Photography by Tim Clinch
Property: Le Manoir aux Quat'Saisons, Oxfordshire
Snow Queen lyrics inspired by Todhunter Earle
Todhunter Earle
Chelsea Reach 79-89 Lots Road
London SW10 0RN
T: 020 7349 9999
F: 020 7349 0410

PAGE 116
Photography by Tim Clinch
Property: Floriana Restaurant, London
PAGE 117
Photography by Fritz von der Schulenburg
Property: Cadogan Place, London

DIRECTORY

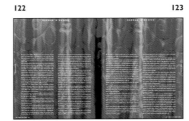

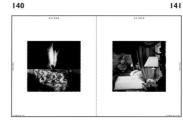

CREDITS AND CONTACTS

DIRECTORY

PHOTOGRAPHY

150   151

PAGES 150-151
Photography by Dominic Blackmore
Property: St John's Westminster in
London
Developer: Ballymore Properties
Hunt Hamilton Zuch
Studio G2 Chelsea Reach
79-89 Lots Road
London SW10 0RN
T: 020 7795 1113
F: 020 7795 1114

152   153

PAGES 152-153
Photography by Mark Luscombe-White
Charles Bateson Design Consultants
18 King's Road St Margaret's
Twickenham
Middlesex TW1 2QS
UK
T: 020 8892 3141
F: 020 8891 6483
charles.bateson@btinternet.com

154   155

PAGES 154-155
Photography by Henry Wilson
Architect: John Pawson
The Interior Archive Limited
15 Grand Union Centre, West Row
London W10 5AS
T: 020 7370 0595
F: 020 8960 2695
www.interiorarchive.com

156   157

PAGES 156-157
*Photography by Simon Upton @ The
Interior Archive Limited*
Property: Domenico Dolce and Stefano
Gabbana's Milanese Villa, Italy
Courtesy of designer Dolce & Gabbana

CREDITS AND CONTACTS

158   159

160   161

162   163

164   165

PAGE 165
Words by Carolynne Murphy

ACKNOWLEDGEMENTS

166   167

PAGE 166
Words by Carolynne Murphy
PAGE 167
Closing poetry by Vincent Robert

168   IBC
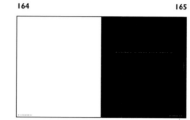

RESEARCH AND EDITORIAL CONCEPTS:
Carolynne Murphy

ART DIRECTION AND GRAPHIC
DESIGN:
Fiona Forsyth

REPRODUCTION, PRE-PRESS AND
PRINTING:
Hyway Printing Group, London

BINDING:
Hunter & Foulis, Edinburgh

TYPEFACES:
Bodoni and Gill Sans

PAPER:
Jacket: HannoArt Matt 170gsm
Cover: HannoArt Matt 130gsm
End papers: Colorplan 140gsm
Text: HannoArt Matt 150gsm

SCANNER:
Screen SG8060

SCREENING:
200 lpi

PRESS:
Heidelberg 102

INKS:
VanSon

INK SEQUENCE:
KMCY

PLATES:
Fuji VPS-E

I have written this with great care.

Leaving enough room for you to read between the lines.

I am indebted to the following friends for moving my dream:

The designers for standing side by side and dancing, just once, to the same tune.

The photographers for capturing the stars.

Fiona Forsyth for being the constant.

Karen Howes for sweeping a pathway and placing her Interior Archives at my feet.

London First for helping to deliver the message.

Alan Jones at Hyway for providing simply the best transport.

Eddie Holmes and Ian Milne for having an infinite appreciation of complex design dialects.

Stanley Kekwick at Art Books International for playing postman.

Louise Page, Ian McLellan, David Browning and Barrie Gill for their support.

'Fourth Angel' Film Productions for inviting *Interior Elite* onto their Pinewood set.

Sheila, Cil, Fi, Bam, Julie and Paula for retrieving my loudest laugh.

My brother John for proving that if we all did the things we are capable of doing we would literally astound ourselves.

My mum, Muriel Evans, for teaching me to smell the flowers.

My dad, Derrick, for erasing the word 'can't' from my vocabulary.

Stuart, Kimberley and Lewis for reminding me to ask and answer the question 'why?'

Michael for grounding me when the dream was a nightmare.

ACKNOWLEDGEMENTS